EXPLORING CHRISTIANITY

Exploring Christianity

Answers to the Questions Every Christian Asks

R. ALEX CHAPMAN

R. Alex Chapman Publishing

Dedications

This book is dedicated to:

The saints who gather at Georges Creek Baptist Church, whose questions and deep desire to grow in their knowledge of the Lord prompted a sermon series, a podcast, and now a book. Thank you for your support and your prayers. It's a joy to pastor you and grow alongside you.

This book is also dedicated to:

Anna, my wonderful wife. None of what I do on a weekly basis would be possible without you and your support. You're a lightning rod that keeps me grounded. You're a shelter for refuge. You're an anchor in the midst of a raging storm and crashing waves. You're my best friend and the love of my life, so this one's for you, Tiny.

Finally, this book is dedicated to:

My two sons, Judah and Ezra. Boys, I pray that one day, when you can read, you'll read this book and strengthen your faith. Never be afraid to ask the hard questions; they're never too much for the Lord. Never be afraid to listen to other sides or other perspectives. Never be afraid to engage any question. Ask good questions, think, and know that in the end, the Lord and His Word will prove true.

May your Scriptures be my pure delight, so that I am not deceived in them and do not lead others astray in interpreting them.

-Augustine, *Confessions*

Contents

Foreword

It is my privilege to have known Rev. Alex Chapman since 2020. We met at a pastor's gathering in Easley, SC, after being connected through a mutual friend. Alex and I have shared a passion for expository preaching and defending historic Christian doctrines that are constantly under attack in these theologically anemic times in which we live. Alex is a dedicated pastor, husband, father, and friend.

As our friendship grew, Alex and I found ourselves facing the same problem in our congregations, as well as many "bible belt" churches: biblical illiteracy. While many pastors bemoan their congregations' lack of understanding of basic Bible doctrine, Alex Chapman went on the offensive in writing this book. Alex seeks to offer biblical insight into many common questions Christians ask and face. He does not simply give his opinion in *Exploring Christianity* but rather points his readers to the ultimate and final source of truth, the Holy Scriptures. With the theological prowess of a scholar and the down-to-earth touch of a local pastor, Alex offers deep insight into the Scriptures for those filled with biblical questions.

When I was approached by Alex to write his foreword, I was touched in my heart and encouraged in the fight against biblical illiteracy. By reading and studying *Exploring Christianity*, one is provided with rock-solid, biblical answers to some serious questions. To those who may be struggling in their faith or simply desiring to know more of God's Word, I cannot overemphasize the importance of studying this great work.

In Christ,
Dr. J. Bradley Starnes
Senior Pastor
Cedar Shoals Baptist Church
September 22, 2023

Introduction

I never thought I would be a Christian, let alone the pastor of a Southern Baptist Church, but God has a sense of humor. After the Lord saved me and made it clear to me that He wanted me to pastor, I prayed that He would send me anywhere other than the Bible belt, but once again, God had other plans for my life. I didn't want to serve in the Bible-belt because even though many people think it's easier to pastor in the South, where churches are on every corner, I knew it would be much more difficult thanks to the plague of nominal Christianity. You see, pretty much everybody in the South thinks they are Christians simply because they acknowledge that God is real, or because they were baptized as a child, or because they have attended the same church their whole lives; however, far too many of them have never truly repented of their sins and trusted in Christ alone for salvation, meaning, they aren't really Christians. They think they are, but they're not.

One of the main reasons they are so misguided is because for far too long, preachers have been more focused on increasing their numbers than they have been on edifying the sheep. Sermons became little more than feel-good, motivational speeches filled with stories and jokes meant to entertain people. So, for years, people gathered with the church, but they weren't being fed. As a result of this, people became biblically illiterate. Dr. Brad Starnes has wisely noted that biblical illiteracy is the single greatest problem in the church today. By biblical illiteracy,

Dr. Starnes means not just an unfamiliarity with Scripture but also an inability to understand and interpret Scripture.

I encountered this firsthand as I began serving as pastor of Georges Creek Baptist Church. Our people truly did love the Lord and desired to serve Him well, to be part of His mission here on earth, but so many didn't know how to read and interpret the Bible correctly. It wasn't their fault. They had just never been taught how to before. One of the first series I taught during our Wednesday evening gatherings was on How to Read and Interpret the Bible. With that series serving as a solid foundation, our people were beginning to study Scripture confidently on their own, but they still had questions. They were hungry for the Word and wanted to know what the Bible said about a variety of topics. So I started a Sunday evening series called Ask Pastor Alex. The idea was that people in the church would submit their questions about Christianity or the Bible or theology, and I would answer them during our Sunday evening gathering. These meetings proved to be beneficial, and people were grateful that they were beginning to get answers to questions they had been asking for years.

However, we restructured our services, so things changed. We began to have Gospel Groups on Sunday evenings, mean-ing we no longer did the Ask Pastor Alex series. But people still had questions. People were consistently asking me what the Bible says about this or that or what Christianity teaches about various topics. As their pastor, I wanted to answer every question they had, but I struggled to figure out the best way to answer them. I could send an email or make a phone call. I could visit them at their house or take time after one of our services. I didn't really like any of those options, though, be-cause 1) it would take a good deal of time, and 2) I knew that if they wanted to know the answers to those questions, then other people would want to know too. I needed a better way to answer the questions every Christian was asking and answer them in a way that would be accessible to the most people possible.

So, in the spring of 2023, I started the Ask Pastor Alex Podcast. The goal was the same as with the series: give people an opportunity to submit questions and answer them in a simple, biblical manner. More than anything, I wanted people to see that the Bible has the answers they need, that the Word of God has the answers to the questions we ask, and to teach them how to use the Bible to answer their questions. I didn't know if anybody would even listen to the podcast. I had no idea it would come to have so many faithful supporters and listeners, people who tune in every week and listen to that week's episode, and so many people who submit questions. I never thought I would receive all the grateful emails and messages from people expressing how thankful they were for the podcast and so happy to have answers to their questions. The Lord has been good to us.

But not everybody likes technology. Many people, myself included, still prefer books, actual books that you hold in your hands. So, I began to consider turning the podcast into a book. The idea was that a book would be a helpful resource at the ready. For instance, a person might listen to a podcast episode on how certain books ended up in the Bible while others did not. Maybe later, they're talking to someone about the topic but struggling to remember everything they listened to. They don't want to return and relisten to the episode, but if they had a book, they could open up to the chapter and reference it. That was what prompted me to pursue writing this book. I was excited by the idea of people using this book as a ready resource to answer their questions and their friends, family, coworkers, etc.

Even though I graduated top of my class at North Greenville University, where I earned a B.A. in Christian Studies, and even though I graduated in the top 2% of my class at The Southern

Baptist Theological Seminary, where I earned an M.Div. in Christian Ministry, this book is not an academic book. That's by design. I love academia, but I want this book to be accessible to all people. On the podcast, I talk to the audience exactly how I would talk to any one of my church members. Since this book stems from the podcast, I write the same way I would talk to anyone who might ask me any of these questions during a conversation. So the informal writing is meant to make these questions accessible to all people. Not only is the informal writing by design, but also so is the chapter length. I've tried to answer each question as concisely as possible. Please understand that for many of these questions, entire books have been written in response, so much more could be said for any given question. My goal is not to answer each question exhaustively but sufficiently. I write for the people in the pews.

The book's goal is simple: to use the Bible to answer questions that most Christians have asked and wondered about. It's my hope that this book will help correct the problem of biblical illiteracy in the church. By reading this book, not only will you have many of your own questions answered, but you will also learn how to read and interpret the Bible, how to think biblically, how to pay attention to important details in Scripture, how to connect different stories in Scripture, and how to reject assumptions in search of truth. You'll also learn some interesting facts from church history as well as many cool insights from Scripture that often get missed. You might not agree with everything I say in the book, and that's okay. However, I want you to understand that I derive my answers from Scripture and stand by them for that reason.

I hope this book grows your love for the Lord, your hunger for His Word, and your desire to keep asking questions and digging for answers.

Soli Deo Gloria,

R. Alex Chapman, September 22, 2023

Chapter 1

How Were People Saved in the Old Testament?

✝

This is a question that people have asked me a number of times at this point in my walk with Christ because there's a lot of confusion about this topic, and people want clarity. When this question was originally submitted to me, the person asked, "How were people saved in the Old Testament considering the fact that Jesus hadn't even been born yet?" First, I just want to say I know what the person meant by "Jesus had not even been born yet." I know the person who submitted this question was thinking that Jesus had not yet been born of the Virgin Mary. He had not taken on human flesh. He was not living amongst us here on earth. However, we have to keep in mind that Jesus is eternal. So, while He might not have had human flesh on at that point and been living among us here on earth, He was very much alive because He's always been alive.

The Bible says in John chapter 1:1-3, "In the beginning was the Word and the Word was with God and the Word was

God. He was in the beginning with God. All things were made through him, and without him was not anything made that was made." The Bible says there that Jesus has always existed. He was present with the Father and the Holy Spirit in the beginning, and everything made was made through Jesus. So, Jesus has always been alive.

The second part of the question is, "How were people saved in the Old Testament then?" We know as Christians we're saved by Jesus and His life of righteousness, His substitutionary death on the cross, and His resurrection and ascension. It's all about Jesus. When we repent of our sins and put our trust in Him, His righteousness is attributed to us through faith, and His death is counted as our own through faith. So, how were the people in the Old Testament or the Old Covenant times saved?

There are two common misconceptions about this today. The first is that people were saved by offering up sacrifices to God. Many Christians still believe this today. They believe that the way people were saved during the Old Covenant times was by offering up sacrifices for their sins. However, the Bible clearly demonstrates this idea to be wrong. In Hebrews 10:4, we read, "For it is impossible for the blood of bulls and goats to take away sins." Contrary to the popular belief that people might have been saved by offering sacrifices in the Old Covenant, the Bible says that the blood of bulls and goats cannot take away sins. In fact, as the chapter continues, we read in verse 11, "Every priest stands daily at his service offering repeatedly the same sacrifices, which can never take away sins."

The Bible is saying there's this laborious, tedious act of having to stand daily and offer these sacrifices. The frustrating part of it is they can't actually take away sins. You see, God, in His grace, provided the people with the sacrificial system to temporarily remove their uncleanness and to appease His wrath temporarily, but the sacrifices were not salvific. *No person has ever been saved through the sacrificial system.*

However, there's another popular suggestion. If it wasn't for the sacrifices, then people must have been saved through obedience, right? They would follow the law and the commandments, and if they could do that, they would be saved, right? No, the Bible addresses this in Galatians chapter 3, beginning in verse 10,

> For all who rely on works of the law are under a curse. For it is written, 'cursed be everyone who does not abide by all things written in the book of the law and do them.' Now it is evident that no one is justified before God by the law, for the righteous shall live by faith. But the law is not of faith, rather the one who does them shall live by them. Christ redeemed us from the curse of the law by becoming a curse for us. For it is written, "cursed is everyone who is hanged on a tree, so that in Christ Jesus the blessing of Abraham might come to the Gentiles, so that we might receive the promised spirit through faith.

The Bible is saying that people who try to keep the law are responsible for keeping the entire law. If they fail to keep even one aspect of the law, they have failed to keep the entire law. Because if you are a transgressor in one area, well then, you've transgressed the entire law (James 2:10). Therefore, it is impossible for us as fallen human creatures to keep the law perfectly. That is beyond our ability. The Bible says in Romans 3:23 that "all have sinned and fall short of the glory of God." We are all sinners. None of us have kept the law perfectly. The only person who has been able to keep the law perfectly is Jesus, and praise God for that.

So again, we get back to this question: well then, how were they saved? How were people in the Old Covenant times saved? The answer is very simple: it's by grace through faith in

Christ. That might seem strange at first because you might be thinking, as the person who submitted this question did, "But Jesus was not born at that point. He hadn't come to earth. He had not lived his perfect, righteous, obedient life. He had not died his sacrificial, atoning death on the cross. He had not risen from the grave and defeated sin, Satan, death, and all these things. So how is that possible?"

Well, we're going to get into that, but I just want you to understand that it has always been by grace alone through faith alone in Christ alone. We even read this as early as the first book of the Bible. Genesis 15:6 says that "Abraham believed God (the word "believe" is the same word for faith), and it was reckoned to him as righteousness."[1] The word "reckoned" means counted.[2] In other words, God counted (declared) Abraham to be righteous in His sight, *not* because of something he did, *not* because of keeping commandments or by being perfectly obedient, but because he *trusted* in Yahweh. He *believed* in God. He had *faith*.

In fact, Paul uses that example from Genesis 15:6 in his writing in Romans chapter 4 to defend the doctrine of justification by faith, that we are declared righteous in God's sight only by faith. Paul even uses the same word "counted" throughout Romans 4, showing that the way of salvation has been the same in both covenants. We don't earn righteousness; righteousness is *counted* to us through faith in Jesus. Furthermore, the Bible says in Ephesians chapter 2:8, "For by grace you have been saved through faith and this is not your own doing, it is the gift of God." Remember, the Bible said back in Galatians chapter 3 that no one is going to be justified before God or in the eyes of God by keeping the works of the law, by doing the works of the law. That's impossible. It has always been by trusting in God. How does this play out? Especially because, as the person who submitted the question asked, Jesus hadn't yet lived at that point, at least on earth.

The Bible says in Revelation chapter 13:8 that Jesus is the Lamb of God who was slain from the foundation of the world. In other words, God knew before He ever created anything that if He gave people the opportunity to follow Him in obedience or give in to sin, He knew that eventually, we would give in to sin, that we would fall. That's exactly what happened. Therefore, before God ever created anything, He had a plan to redeem His people in Christ Jesus, that He would do for us what we could not do for ourselves. He was going to secure an eternal redemption through His Son.

Think again about Abraham. Abraham knew that he could not offer up enough sacrifices to have an eternal redemption. He knew that there was no way he could be perfectly obedient. If you read Genesis, you know that he wasn't. So, what Abraham was doing was putting all his hope for an eternal salvation in God. He knew the God that he served. He knew Yahweh intimately. He was a friend of God, and he knew that God would one day do something to secure an eternal redemption.

We actually read about that in the book of John. In John 8:56, Jesus tells the religious teachers that Abraham looked forward to Jesus's day with great anticipation. He was looking forward to that day, and he rejoiced. He rejoiced even though he didn't have the full picture. No one in the Old Testament did. They didn't have the full picture of what God was going to do. They had bits of prophecy and revelation that God had given them. They had enough to start getting this fuzzy picture. It was as if they were seeing it through a veil, which Paul picks up on in 2 Corinthians chapter 3, but they were seeing all this through a veil, and they had a general idea of what was going to happen but not the particulars. They knew that God was going to do something, so they looked forward to that day with great joy, anticipation, and rejoicing. Therefore, God would declare them righteous in His sight because they were trusting in Him alone. They had faith in what God was going to do.

A good way to think about salvation in the Old Covenant times versus New Covenant times is the difference between credit and debit. Let's say you wanted to go and purchase something like a fancy TV or some other expensive item. Let's say you don't have the funds readily available but have a credit card. So you use your credit card to buy an expensive item. What you're doing is securing the purchase at that moment with a guarantee that you're going to pay it off later.

Well, that's what God was doing with the Old Covenant saints. He was saying, hey, you are saved in my sight through faith in Me and what I'm going to do in the future. You are righteous in my sight. This salvation is yours, and I'm going to pay it off later at the cross of Christ. In the mind of God, Jesus had already been sacrificed on the cross. Remember, He is the lamb who was slain from the foundation of the world, but the people had to wait for that event to take place in history. So, they were saved on credit.

But everyone is saved on debit after the cross because the payment has already been made. The payment is already in the bank. Jesus has already died on the cross. He has risen from the dead. He's ascended back to the Father. He's in heaven with the Father right now, interceding for His people. When we hear the gospel message, and we're convicted by the Holy Spirit, and God draws us to Him by His grace in such a way that we actually turn from our sins, we put our faith and trust in Christ alone for salvation, then we have that salvation right then and right there and the payment has already been made. We don't have to trust something to take place in the future based on a fuzzy picture. We trust and hope in something that has already taken place in history. So salvation in the Old Covenant is like being saved on credit, and salvation in the New Covenant is like being saved on debit.

The big takeaway from all this is that there has only ever been one way of salvation. There wasn't one way for Old

Covenant saints and another for New Covenant saints. There has never been two ways. There has only ever been one way of salvation, and it has always been by grace alone through faith alone in Christ alone, according to Scripture alone for the glory of God alone.

Chapter 2

Can Christians Be Possessed by Demons?

✝

I'm always curious about what prompts people to submit certain questions, and I have to wonder if this one is just curiosity and intrigue or if it maybe has something to do with the number of movies we see every year that have to do with demon possession. If we want to answer this question, we have to do what we always do: go to the Bible and see what the Word of God has to say on this subject.

It's interesting that Jesus, very early on in His ministry, had interactions with people possessed by demons. In Mark chapter 1, Jesus encounters a person who is possessed by a demon, and Jesus casts that demon out of the person. Also, the longest account of demon possession and exorcism occurs in Mark chapter 5. It's a really famous passage about the Gerasene man who was possessed by not just a demon but many demons. They are called legion because they are many. When you look at this account and the effects that this possession had upon the Gerasene man, it's pretty concerning.

For instance, the Bible says that he possessed supernatural strength (Mark 5:3). Mark 5:4 says that he could not be held by bonds that could break apart chains and any bonds put upon him. Not only that, but he was living in total isolation (Mark 5:3, 5). It says he was in the caves and mountains and was totally alone. Not only that, but Mark 5:5 says that he was always crying and cutting himself. It's really disturbing when you're reading that and you see the effects of this possession on the man, that he is in total isolation and crying constantly. He's harming himself by cutting himself constantly. Then, not only that, but the Bible also indicates that he wasn't in his right mind as he was possessed. He really wasn't himself as he was possessed by these demons because the Bible says that once Jesus actually cast the legion of demons out and the man was free, only then was he in his right mind (Mark 5:15).

When we read an account like that, I can understand why someone would want to know the answer to this question, why they're curious about whether or not Christians can be possessed by demons because nobody wants that, right? That sounds terrible. Isolation, a level of depression that we probably can't even imagine, always crying, self-harming, cutting yourself, not in your right mind. It seems that the demons if they possess a person, gain total control over that person and what that person thinks and does. So, the question is, well, what does the Bible seem to say about Christians? Can that happen to Christians?

We get an answer in 2 Corinthians chapter 6; actually, there are multiple places in the New Testament that give us good reasons to believe that Christians cannot be possessed by demons. 2 Corinthians chapter 6, starting in verse 14, the Bible says, do not be unequally yoked with unbelievers. For what partnership has righteousness with lawlessness? Or what fellowship has light with darkness? What accord has Christ with Belial? Or what portion does a believer share with an unbeliever? What agreement has the temple of God with idols? For we are the temple of the living God. As God said, I will make my dwelling among them and I will walk among them and I will be their God and they shall be my people.

We know that as Christians, we are indwelt by the Holy Spirit of God Himself. We are the temple of the living God, and the living God lives in us. He has indwelt us by His Holy Spirit. The Bible emphasizes here that the Holy Spirit cannot occupy the same space as the demons, as that which is unholy and unrighteous. The darkness has nothing to do with the light.

We even get a further answer in 1 John chapter 4:1-4. The Bible says,

Beloved, do not believe every spirit, but test the spirits to see whether they are from God. For many false prophets have gone into the world. By this, you know the Spirit of God: every spirit that confesses that Jesus Christ has come in the flesh is from God. And every spirit that does not confess Jesus is not from God. This is the Spirit of the Antichrist, which you heard was coming and now is in the world. Little children, you are from God and have overcome them. For He who is in you is greater than he who is in the world.

Notice the contrast there. The Bible says here's how you can tell if a spirit is from the Holy Spirit: they're going to confess that Jesus Christ came in the flesh, that He is the Son of the Living God. Then the Bible also says, but if that's not the case, it's going to be the spirit of the antichrist who comes from the demonic realm, the realm of Satan. The Bible says here that "He who is in [us]," referring there to the Holy Spirit, "is greater than he who is in the world," referring to the spirits of the demonic realm.

Here's the important point for consideration: when the Bible says, "He who is in you," who is it referring to there? If Christians can be possessed by demons, then we would have to ask, is this referring to the Holy Spirit or to a demon who might be possessing a Christian at any given time? That wouldn't make sense. This verse is clearly referring to the Holy Spirit, but if a Christian could actually be possessed by demons at any point, then we would have no idea who this verse is referring to; it could be the Holy Spirit or it could be a demon. The only thing that would make sense is if this is referring **exclusively** to the Holy Spirit and in such a way that it can *never be referring to anyone else*. In other words, it is absolutely impossible for a demon to possess a Christian *because* Christians have the Holy Spirit of God living within them.

Can Christians be possessed by demons? The Bible gives a very clear answer, an emphatic no. Christians cannot be possessed by demons. However, that raises another issue that we should at least touch on very quickly: what about demon *oppression*? Because there is a big difference between being *possessed by demons* and being *oppressed by demons*. As we mentioned before, possession seems to indicate that the demonic spirit has complete control over the person it currently possesses. They would be able to make sure the person is not in their right mind. They would be able to make them commit self-harm, cut themselves constantly, and become severely depressed. They would have control over their speech, thoughts, actions, and all that kind of stuff, right? We know that that can't happen to a Christian, and we praise God for that, but it is also true that Christians can be oppressed or harassed by the realm of the demonic, specifically demonic forces and demons themselves.

If you want a good example of this, just think about Jesus. In Matthew chapter 4, Jesus experiences oppression and harassment by Satan himself. Satan comes to Jesus while He is in the wilderness, and Satan begins to harass Him and tempt Him to the point where Jesus eventually says, get away from me, Satan, and He casts him away. Jesus wasn't possessed by Satan, obviously, but He was being harassed by Satan.

Not only that, but we see an instance of this in the life of the Apostle Paul in 2 Corinthians 12, where Paul explains that he received "a thorn in his flesh." Right after that, he mentions he was "given a messenger from Satan." This "thorn in the flesh, this messenger from Satan," was there to humble Paul to keep him from becoming conceited. So, Paul was absolutely harassed by at least one messenger from Satan, probably many, and oppressed in many ways by the demonic realm as well. To say that Christians can be oppressed by demons is to say that Christians can and will experience harassment by demons, temptation by demons, opposition from demons, and even have to deal with demons seeking to thwart their attempts to follow God and disrupt their ministries and service to God.

Therefore, it is possible for demons to oppress Christians and harass Christians to try to thwart our efforts that God has given us to preach the gospel and expand the kingdom here on earth. The demonic realm can try to confuse Christians, sow seeds of dissension amongst the church, and cause divisions to take place that absolutely can and will happen. But to answer the question very plainly, no, Christians cannot be possessed by demons because we are indwelled by the Holy Spirit of God, and praise God for that.

Chapter 3

What Should We Think About the Asbury Revival?

✝

For those who might not be familiar with the Asbury Revival, Asbury Seminary was having its regular chapel service, and the speaker was giving his message. At the end of the message, he concluded in prayer. Then, it's my understanding that students remained at the chapel and began to pray, which blossomed into more worship songs, prayer, and confession. These things continued for some time, and it was spontaneous and unplanned. At least, it started out that way. People continued to pray and worship for two weeks, and the events there garnered much media attention. People were posting about it on social media, national media, and many other places, making them wonder, "What is happening at Asbury? Is this a true revival? Are we finally seeing another true revival in America, not one that's planned at your typical Southern Baptist Church where it's like, hey, we have a revival planned for November, and it's going to be from these days to these days, but just a true, genuine revival from God?" Therefore, it's right and appropriate to be asking questions like this. What should we, as Christians, think about the Asbury revival?

First, I can't tell you what to think about the Asbury revival. I don't want to tell you what to think. I want to *help* you think, and I want to be able to give you tools and resources for thinking and maybe give you some ideas for how to think through this. But at the end of the day, you should do your own research. You should be well informed. You should look to the Scriptures and form your own opinion based on those things rather than just taking what I tell you and running with that. I don't ever want to tell you what to think, but I want to help you think through these issues. As we come to a situation like this, with the Asbury revival, we need to understand that there are typically two common responses that happen when you hear about a revival or some great movement of God. They're on the opposite ends of the spectrum from each other.

The first group hears about a revival, and this great movement of God that's taking place, and one of the most common responses is immediate dismissal. This is kind of the cynical, overly critical group. They are very staunch, and they like things nice and neat and orderly and like to try to have everything work in a certain way. When they hear about a revival, they are quick to dismiss it and say, "How can you be so foolish to believe that this is actually a true revival and a true movement from God?" It's kind of a condescending attitude like you should know better. You should know that this isn't a true revival. That kind of thing does not happen anymore. If it does, it looks like this rather than like that. So, the first common response is immediate dismissal.

However, there's an equally unwise response that's just as common, and that's immediate affirmation, immediate approval. Many people fall into this category. They immediately put forward their opinions of the situation, and they say, "Of course, this is a true revival. How dare you question this true movement of God!" Well, how do you know it's a true revival? "Because it is. Clearly, it is, right?" They give their immediate affirmation to this and their immediate approval, and, like the first group, they also have a condescending attitude. The group that is quick to dismiss looks down on you *intellectually*, like how could you be so foolish? However, the group that is quick to affirm looks down on you *spiritually*, and they're saying, "How can you deny this true spiritual movement of God that's taking place? You should know better than that. If you were more in line with Christ or if you were holier, then of course you would immediately say that this is a true movement of God." I've even seen some pastors and prominent people talk about the fact that judging a spiritual movement from afar says more about you than about that movement.

Meanwhile, I'm asking, "Can we just maybe take a middle ground? Is there something so wrong with taking the middle ground?" It's unwise to immediately dismiss what could potentially be a true movement of God, but it's equally unwise to give your immediate affirmation and approval of something without any serious level of discernment, critical thinking, or evaluation.

Those things aren't unbiblical. It's not wrong to question and ask good critical questions and to investigate something before you give your approval to it. That's biblical. Think about Acts chapter 17 when Paul is in Berea, and he's preaching the Word and sharing the gospel, and the Bible says that the people were "eagerly receiving what he was saying." (Acts 17:11). They were eager about it. They were excited about Paul's teaching and about him showing them that Jesus is the Messiah. But what did they do? They used discernment. They asked very critical questions. They went to the Scriptures because they wanted to verify that what Paul was saying was in line with the Scriptures. They wanted to make sure that it was biblical.

Well, I'm wondering, why can't we take that same response here? What's so wrong with taking a discerning response? A discerning response is the best response and at least maybe the most biblical and wise response we can take in a situation like this. We should take the Berean approach and look in Scripture and say, "Okay, are the things that happened at Asbury in line with what the Bible says about true revivals, and are the things that went on there in line with a true movement of God?" There is absolutely nothing wrong with asking those types of questions.

In fact, I think it's very helpful and very biblical because the Bible also warns us in 1 John chapter 4, "Beloved, do not believe every spirit." But what does the Bible tell us to do? "But test the spirits to see whether they are from God, for many false prophets have gone out to the world." Well, there's the Bible telling us exactly how to handle the Asbury revival. Don't be immediately dismissive of it. Don't be immediately affirmative of it or approving of it. Rather, test the spirits because not everything that claims to be a spiritual movement is a true spiritual movement. That doesn't mean that this one is not. It just means test the spirits. Not every spirit is from God. That's the approach we need to take because we need to look at the Asbury revival and ask some really good questions.

I've seen a lot of stuff that is trying to put it down. I've seen some reports of the leaders and some negative things about them. I've seen some things about the message itself. These are important issues to bring up, but at the end of the day, we have a responsibility as Christians to give people the benefit of the doubt. Let's not just be dismissive because we like being overly critical, but also not be immediately supportive and affirmative just because we want this to be a true revival. I think we look at what's going on. We see if it aligns with Scripture. We look at what is being taught there and said there at the revival. We look at the movement itself and what is going on, and we begin to ask very important questions about whether that aligns with what the Scripture says a true revival is and what a true revival looks like.

We need to remember that all true revivals are known in time, so we don't have to come to some sort of conclusion even right now. I think it's okay to say, "I'm not sure if this is a true revival or not." I'm not saying that it's not. I'm not saying that it is. I'm saying, "I don't know." Time will tell. Time is going to show us what to make of this revival and its long-term effects. Is it going to be something that dies out and has no lasting impact on the people who were there, the people who continue to be there, the area, and the school, or is it going to be something that has long-term effects and doesn't just stay confined to one place but something that spreads across our own country, across the world, that has long-term effects on the students, the people who were there, the staff who continues to be there, the people in the area. We will see in time what to make of the Asbury revival.

So what do we do now? If you haven't been there, you must admit you don't know. You've seen good and bad reports. You've seen a lot of good videos being posted. You've seen a lot of critical things being posted. At the end of the day, we say, I wasn't there, so I don't know. We can be fairly confident that there were certainly people there who experienced a true revival, who were awakened to the reality of their sin and were convicted by the Holy Spirit. Maybe they even turned from their sins and trusted in Christ for the first time, and now they are giving their lives to Jesus.

We can also be confident some people there were already true Christians, but maybe they were lax in their faith or not very committed. When they went to this revival or whatever is going on here, they experienced an awakening spiritually and became aware of the fact that they had become lax in their faith and were awakened to the reality of ongoing sin in their life, their need to commit to the spiritual disciplines and grow closer to Christ. They had a renewed fear of the Lord and a desire to be in His Word and live in accordance with His Word. I feel very confident saying that there were people there who experienced those things.

I also feel just as confident saying that I think there were many people there who maybe went for the wrong reasons or just went strictly out of curiosity and not to experience a movement of God. I think there were probably some people there who genuinely dedicated themselves to prayer and worship, and I think there were probably some people there who were just trying to keep this revival going as long as they possibly could. I think both things can be true at the same time without having to dismiss the whole thing entirely or approve of the whole thing entirely.

What can we do as Christians? Well, I think one of the best things we can do is pray. That's always one of the best things we can do because God works in prayer and through prayer, and He can do great things through the prayers of His people. One of the best things that we can do is pray, "Lord, if this was a true revival, I pray that You will make that evident. I pray that it won't just be confined to Asbury Seminary, but I pray that it will begin to spread to the community and then the state and then the nation and then the world and that there will be revivals taking place all across our world. I pray, Lord, that as a result of this revival, You would bring people to a true saving faith in Christ and that those who were already Christians would have a renewed commitment to Christ and His Kingdom and the gospel and Your purposes. Lord, if this was not a true revival, I pray that some good will come from it, that You will use something that might not be genuine to bring about something that is good. I pray, Lord, that if this was not a true revival, at least the amount of attention it received in the media and on social media will awaken people to their need for Christ and our need as a people for revival. Because of their interest in what happened at Asbury, I pray that people will seek out a local church in their own community and begin to go to that church where they might hear the gospel preached and experience the conviction of the Holy Spirit."

We can pray that even if this was not a true revival, the Lord would use it to bring about good from it, which we know that He does. He is able to bring about good even from bad situations. The wisest thing for us to do in this situation is to be discerning and to be prayerful. Those two things are always good responses.

Chapter 4

How Do We Know Which Old Testament Laws Apply to Christians Today?

†

Jesus says in Matthew 5:18, "For truly, I say to you, until heaven and earth pass away, not an iota, not a dot, will pass away from the Law until all is accomplished." Given Matthew 5:18, how can we look at the various sets of laws in the Old Testament and understand which are still to be upheld and which are no longer applicable? That's a question that a lot of people have wondered about as Christ followers. It's appropriate as Christians to ask, "When I read the Old Testament and specifically the law sections of the Old Testament, how do I know if the laws that I'm reading apply today?"

Different people answer this question in many different ways. Some are more helpful than others. One unhelpful answer that you hear sometimes is that none of it applies today because now we are under grace and not under the law. Yes, the Bible says that we are under grace, not law, but what does that mean? Because keep in mind the law was never given for salvific purposes. God did not give the Israelites the law and say, "If you keep this, you will be saved." That's not how it worked. Remember, when God gave the people of Israel the law, He had already saved them and delivered them from their slavery in Egypt, an Old Testament event that serves as a paradigm for salvation. Therefore, the law was never given for salvific or legalistic purposes, as in, do this to be saved. The law was given as a set of rules for the people of Israel to know how to live as God's people in the world. He was saying, "You are a nation that I have saved unto myself, that I've called out of Egypt, and this is how you are to live and be governed as My people who are going to be living in the promised land."

Of course, there were blessings for obedience and curses for disobedience, which related specifically to the fact that the Israelites were under the Old Covenant. It's important to remember that Christians are part of the New Covenant. The blessings for obedience and curses for disobedience were specifically tailored and related to the Old Covenant. So the view that none of the law applies today is not only unhelpful but fails to fully grasp the purpose of the Law in the first place. It's also helpful to remember Jesus' own summary of the law was that the entire law could be summarized in basically two phrases: love God and love other people. If you do those two things, then you're fulfilling the *purposes* of the law.

Then, there is another response. The first group says Christians should get rid of the entire law. There's a second group that says Christians need to think about the law in terms of three categories. The ceremonial laws relate to Israel's worship: the feasts, the festivals, and the sacrifices are all ceremonial laws. These ceremonial laws, they claim, have all been fulfilled by Christ. Praise God, that is true. We know that we don't offer sacrifices today, and we don't have to observe these festivals and feasts and all that today because Jesus is the once for all time sacrifice (Hebrews 9:26-28), and the Bible specifically says in the book of Hebrews that there are therefore now no more sacrifices that could be made for sins because Jesus has been offered up as the once for all time sacrifice for our sins (Hebrews 10:18). So ceremonial laws are the first category of laws, but then the second category refers to civil laws. The civil laws were specifically related to Israel's government and how they were to govern themselves as a nation. These laws, they claim, no longer apply to Christians today because the people of God today do not exist as a nation; therefore, these laws are no longer relevant for Christians today. The final category is moral laws. As you can imagine, moral laws have to do with Christian character or the character of a God follower. They would say that these laws still apply today because they are rooted in God's character and meant to be reflected by God's people.

These three categories can be both helpful and unhelpful. For instance, they are helpful in giving us categories by which we can think about the laws when we read them. When reading certain laws, we can have a loose guide to see where certain laws fall in a category. This means that the categories help us process what we're reading. However, the categories can also be unhelpful too. For instance, some laws could fit into multiple categories, so you have difficulty determining whether this is a civil or ceremonial law. Is this ceremonial or moral? If it seems like it could fit into multiple categories, then you don't know if it applies or not. Not only that but also there are other laws that don't seem to fit into any one of the three categories. For instance, what do you do with dietary laws? When the Bible says, don't eat this particular kind of food, that's not ceremonial. That's not really civil, and it's probably not moral. So, that doesn't really fit into any one of those three categories. What do you do with the dietary laws? Therefore, these categories can be both helpful and unhelpful.

To further answer this question, let's get into some particulars here and offer ways to think through the laws as we read them. First, when we're reading the law section of the Bible, we always need to be trying to get at the heart or the spirit of the law. We need to be asking, "Why did God give this law in the first place? What's its purpose? What's the intent behind it?" We think like this because that's how Jesus thought about the law, and that's how He taught us to think about the law.

Think back to Jesus's Sermon on the Mount. Jesus was constantly trying to correct the Pharisees from just thinking about the letter of the law and trying to get them thinking about the heart or the spirit of the law. So, the law says you shall not murder. The Pharisees said, "Okay, we won't go and commit the physical act of murder, and that means we are good. We are righteous law-keepers." But Jesus says, actually, the heart behind this law, the spirit of the law, is if you have anger in your heart towards your brother, you're going to suffer the same punishment as the one who goes through with the physical act of murder because every murder begins in the heart (Matthew 5:21-26). The law also says, "You shall not commit adultery." The Pharisees said, "Okay, we're not going to have a sexual interaction with anyone who is not our spouse. We are righteous law-keepers." But then Jesus says, actually, the spirit behind that law, the heart of it is even if you look at another person with lustful intent in your heart, you've already committed adultery because every adulterous act starts in the heart (Matthew 5:27-30).

Jesus was constantly pointing people to the heart and the importance of the heart. Therefore, when we're reading the law, we need to be trying to get at the spirit or the heart behind that law. For example, just think about a couple of laws. There's a famous law that talks about not wearing clothing that is made up of mixed material. "You shall not wear cloth of wool and linen mixed together" (Deuteronomy 22:11). People like to point that out today, and they'll say, "Well, why do Christians not hold to this law, but they do hold to other aspects of the law?" They think it's hypocritical. They think we're picking and choosing.

So, let's think about this. What is the purpose or the spirit of that law? Why did God give that law in the first place? If you read the context and see what's going on, it becomes clear that the primary reason God gave that law to the Israelites was so that His people would be distinct from the surrounding culture. The other cultures, apparently, wore mixed materials quite often, and you could see that their clothing was made up of more than one material. So, God tells His people, don't do that. Why? Not because it's morally wrong, not because it's ceremonial or civil or anything like that. His desire was for His people to be distinct from the surrounding cultures. That's the spirit of the law. The principle of the law is that God's people are to be distinct from the surrounding cultures.

So then, we ask as Christians today, "How does that apply to us today?" Well, we would say that still applies because Jesus even said that we're to be in the world, but not of the world (John 15:18-20). His people are to be different from those around them. Therefore, when we read the law about mixed clothing, we would ask, as Christians, "How can I be distinct from those around me? How can I be distinct as a Christian, as a person of God?" What you'll find is that there are tons of applications for that, about what you watch and don't watch, about where you go and don't go, what you do and don't do, how you speak, how you treat people, what you love, what you disregard. There are all sorts of applications of that principle, but it all stems from the principle and the spirit of that law: God's people are supposed to be distinct.

There's another law in Leviticus 19 that says in verses 9-10, "When you reap the harvest of your land, you shall not reap your field right up to its edge, neither shall you gather the gleaning after your harvest. And You shall not strip your vineyard bare, neither shall you gather the fallen grapes of your vineyard. You shall leave them for the poor and for the sojourner: I am the Lord your God." This is another law where many Christians today would say, "Well, I don't really farm, so how does this have anything to do with me today? I can't even apply this if I wanted to." But, remember, we have to ask, "What's the spirit behind this law? What's the purpose? Why did God give it?" When you begin to read the surrounding context, the principle is something along the lines that Christians should care for the less fortunate. Christians should care for the poor and for the needy, or get more specific: Christians should provide opportunities for the less fortunate to take care of their own needs. That opens up a wide range of applications, doesn't it? It even calls into question a lot of our charitable giving because notice that the people of Israel here weren't harvesting everything and then taking a portion to the poor. They were leaving a portion of their field unreaped so that the poor could come along and do the work and provide for their needs. Rather than just giving the people a handout, they gave them an opportunity.

As Christians seeking to apply this principle, we would begin to ask, "How can I do that in my own life? How can I provide opportunities for the less fortunate in my life and give them an opportunity even to work to provide for their own needs and meet their needs?" There are lots of different ways that you can make applications of that. But when you're reading the law, the most important thing you can do is try to get at the spirit of the law and the reason why God gave it in the first place. When you can get at that principle, then you can begin to make applications for the Christian life. You'll be surprised when you read the law how much of it actually applies as opposed to how much of it probably doesn't apply. You'll be shocked to find how much of it is still relevant and applies to Christians today.

To summarize, it's helpful to think through the intent, the purpose, the spirit, and the heart of the law. A lot of times when you're having this conversation with people, people focus on the law because they want to do a bit of a gotcha technique like, oh, hey, people get tattoos today, but they condemn homosexual relationships, or people eat this type of food today, but they condemn homosexual relationships and things like that. They think that Christians are picking and choosing and that we're being hypocritical. However, that's just not the case. We're actually seeking to apply the principles of the law to our lives.

We also must consider the full biblical witness on these issues because consider the dietary laws. With the dietary laws, God says don't eat this type of food. In the New Testament, Jesus fulfills that and does away with it. It just requires a little bit of reading. In Acts chapter 10, Peter is hungry. He wants to eat some food. God tells him to eat, and Peter refuses by saying he's not going to eat anything unclean and common. God says, don't call something unclean and common that I have declared to be clean. God was announcing His approval of all the foods that were previously banned. If you want to be more specific about this, in Mark chapter 7:19, Jesus specifically "declares all food clean."

So, when you're reading the law in the Old Testament, something in the New Testament often supersedes what was previously given. Previously, God restricted certain foods, but in the New Testament, Jesus announces all food is clean. Therefore, we aren't trying to be hypocritical. We're trying to be consistent with the message of the Bible. At the end of the day, it's important to remember that the law cannot save you.

No amount of keeping the law can save you. Even if you were to try to keep all of it, you would fail. We are dependent upon Jesus and his grace alone for our salvation.

We need to remember that Jesus fulfilled the entire law and praise God for that. We don't have to meticulously uphold every law, and if we fail, then all of a sudden, we're doomed. We are reliant on the fact that Jesus has already fulfilled the law on our behalf. He has kept the law on our behalf. Now, when we repent of our sins, and we put our trust in him, His righteous obedience is counted to us through faith. This means we are declared right in the eyes of God, not because of our works, but because of what Jesus has done for us and the fact that we've trusted in him. The other thing to remember is that it's not helpful to dismiss the entire law because there are still many parts of it that are incredibly relevant and applicable to the Christian life today.

The laws require a careful reading and a discerning spirit that gets after the spirit and heart of the law and tries to apply the various laws appropriately. It's also important to remember that there's a bad attitude towards the law today where many Christians look down on it and want to be dismissive of it and do away with it. Interestingly, though, you don't find that in the Bible at all. Some of the longest Psalms in the Bible are written about how great the law is. The Israelites loved the law. They rejoiced in the law because it was rooted in the character of God. Though it was impossible for them to keep, and it showed them their need for someone to come and keep it for them on their behalf, they still loved the law of God at the end of the day. Therefore, we should love the law of God while understanding that Jesus has fulfilled it on our behalf. It makes us even more worshipful because we're praising God for this great work that he has done in Christ for us.

The last thing I'll say is we aren't trying to pick and choose which laws to uphold and which laws to dismiss. We're trying to be discerning and ask, "Is this something that was specifically tailored to the government of Israel or something related to the Old Covenant? Or is this something that is applicable for all time because it is revealing the moral character either of God himself or the moral character He desires His people to have in the world?" When it comes to thinking about the law, the most helpful thing I can tell you is to understand Jesus fulfilled the law. Jesus told us the summary of the law was to love God and to love others. Jesus told us to read the law by looking for the spirit of the law, trying to discern the purpose and intent of the law, and then make appropriate applications based on that.

Chapter 5

Should Christians Believe in Ghosts?

✝

It's an interesting question, especially given the number of TV shows that are currently on air about ghost hunting and paranormal activity and considering the number of movies that come out every year that have to do with hauntings and some sort of paranormal activity. I've gotten this question many times from people who have asked me if I believe in ghosts. It might surprise people to hear that my answer is usually, what do you mean by ghosts? Because we have to be careful about how we answer this question.

So, what do you mean by ghosts? For instance, if you are talking about and referring to ghosts in the sense that most of our popular culture refers to, then no, we shouldn't believe in that type of ghost. The popular idea of ghosts in our culture today is of a spirit or a disembodied spirit of a deceased human being, someone who actually lived a life on earth and then died. For some reason, their spirit remained after death and continued to be present, usually in the location where they died or somewhere near there. If that's what you mean by a ghost, then the answer is no, absolutely not. Christians should not believe in that type of ghost because the Bible teaches that when a person dies, their soul either goes to a place of comfort or a place of torment.

The Bible tells us that when a Christian dies, someone who has repented of their sins, they've trusted in Jesus for salvation, they've received the eternal life that Jesus offers as a free gift to those who trust in Him when that person dies, the Bible says, "Yes, we are of good courage, and we would rather be away from the body and at home with the Lord (2 Corinthians 5:8). Absent from the body, at home with the Lord. So, we know that believers' souls go immediately into Jesus's presence. We don't get our resurrection bodies at that time. We aren't physically resurrected, but our spirits, our souls, are in the presence of Jesus and will remain there until He returns, and we receive the physical resurrection body and are ushered into the final judgment and then glory.

Well, for the unbeliever who dies, the Bible actually says that their souls go to a place of torment. There's a really great example of this in the Bible. If you go to Luke chapter 16, you see Jesus' story where He's talking about the rich man and Lazarus. We know that Lazarus was a poor man, and when he died, he was taken to Abraham's bosom, which is that place of comfort. However, when the rich man died, he was taken to a place called Hades. Hades is not hell, but it is a precursor to hell.[3] It is a place where the souls or the spirits of unbelievers go and immediately begin to experience torment that will continue until the final judgment, where they, too, will receive a physical body, and then they will be cast into the lake of fire, which is hell. The Bible very clearly teaches that when humans die, the souls of believers go to be with Jesus in heaven or in a place called Abraham's bosom, which is probably just another name for heaven, and the souls of unbelievers go to this place called Hades, which is a place of torment. We know that is the

case. Therefore, biblically speaking, it is impossible for someone to die and then their soul to remain here on earth in
the form of a spirit or a ghost who would then communicate,
haunt, or do things like that.

Now, I say this is a qualified answer and one that we must
be very particular about because I believe that ghosts are real.
You might be thinking, "But, Pastor, didn't you just contradict
yourself? You just told us all the reasons we shouldn't believe
in ghosts." I was talking about a specific type of ghost, the
"Hollywood ghost." However, biblically speaking, Christians
should believe that ghosts are real. Even the disciples of Jesus
seem to have believed in ghosts. When they were out on the
sea in the midst of a storm and saw Jesus walking on water,
they were terrified and shouted out, "It's a ghost!" (Matthew
14:26).

However, the type of ghosts they believed in and the type
that Christians should continue to believe in is a particular
kind of ghost because the Bible warns us very clearly that there
are demonic forces and demonic spirits, and those demonic
spirits can absolutely 100% appear as ghosts. In fact, you look
in the Bible, and you see plenty of examples of demonic spirits
trying to corrupt the work of God, trying to deceive the people
of God, and trying to cause harm to the mission of God. They
are a pestering force where they are active in the world, and
they like to invoke fear and torment. Biblically speaking, those
are the types of ghosts that we should believe are real and have
very good evidence to believe are real.

Then there's this other follow-up question. What about the
fact that some people claim to have seen ghosts of real people
who lived? What about psychics and people who claim that
they can communicate with people who have died and get real
answers and information that only that person who died would
know about? What about these instances where maybe someone that you know or maybe you personally have lost a loved

one, and you believe that they've appeared to you and things like this? What about ghosts that don't necessarily appear to be evil but in some ways appear to be a pleasant force and things like that? Well, all of those are legitimate questions and concerns, but we should remember that 2 Corinthians 11:14-15 talks about the fact that demonic forces often appear as angels of light and servants of righteousness.

This means it makes really good sense for demonic forces to appear as pleasant spirits. One of the best ways that they can appear as angels of light, servants of righteousness, and really do a lot of emotional harm and damage to people is to appear as someone who really did live and exist and deceive people into thinking that they are that actual person, the spirit or the ghost, the soul, the remainder, whatever you want to call it, of that person who actually lived. In this way, these demonic forces are leading many people astray because people are beginning to believe more in a paranormal realm rather than thinking in a demonic realm. Not only that, but people are turning to psychics and mediums and ghost hunters and things like that rather than turning to the Lord and seeking out what the Word says. Furthermore, a lot of people who have been convinced that these are the souls of their loved ones are being cruelly deceived by demonic forces and spirits.

So, that's the clearest answer that I can give on whether or not Christians should believe in ghosts. The answer is yes, but not the Hollywood ghost, not the type of ghost that would be the remaining soul or spirit of a real person who has died. However, we should absolutely believe in ghosts who are demonic spirits who are seeking to deceive, who are seeking to do harm, who are seeking to confuse, and who are seeking to terrify and frighten.

Knowing this now, Christians should not go to psychics or mediums to seek their advice about a loved one who's passed away. We should also be really careful about what we're watching and exposing ourselves to. A lot of these movies and TV shows do more harm than good because even if it is just a depiction of a Hollywood ghost, it's still opening ourselves up to being influenced by the demonic realm. It's opening ourselves up to being influenced by those evil demonic spirits who are seeking to do harm. So Christians should be very careful about what we actually engage with and expose ourselves to. Should Christians believe in ghosts? Absolutely. By that, you mean demonic spirits seeking to do harm in the world.

Chapter 6

Can Christians Lose Their Salvation?

✝

This question is one that I often wondered about, especially early on in my walk with Christ and shortly after I became a Christian. Many Christians today wonder about that question as well. So, let me just answer this plain and simple: the answer is no. Actually, I'd say the answer is an emphatic no. It's one thing to say that, but let's do what we always do and dig into the Word and see what the Bible has to say about this.

Hebrews 9:12 says, "He (Jesus) entered once for all into the holy places, not by means of the blood of goats and calves but by means of his own blood, thus securing an eternal redemption." In other words, the sacrifices of the Old Covenant were not able to obtain salvation for those who were offering the sacrifices or those for whom the sacrifices were made. However, in contrast to the insufficiency of the Old Covenant sacrifices, Jesus offered up His blood, and by offering His blood, He secured an *eternal redemption*. Praise God for that verse, one of my favorite verses in the Bible. Jesus, when He offered His blood for us, secured an eternal redemption, not a partial redemption or a temporary redemption, an eternal redemption. This means that for any person who has turned from their sins and trusted fully in Jesus and His atoning work, His sacrifice, you have an eternal redemption because Christ secured it with His own blood. Praise God for that.

Not only that, but we also read Ephesians 1:13-14, "In Him, [referring to Jesus], you also, when you heard the word of truth, the gospel of your salvation, believed in Him and were sealed with the promised Holy Spirit, who is the guarantee of our inheritance until we acquire possession of it, to the praise of His glory." This passage is saying that if you are a Christian, you have received the Holy Spirit as a guarantee, a down payment of that future inheritance. The word guarantee is important there. It means God does not give His Holy Spirit to people who will not one day receive the promised inheritance that comes along with the giving of the Holy Spirit.[4] The very fact that we have the Holy Spirit indwelling us right now as believers in Christ guarantees, it is a certainty, that one day we will have that future inheritance that God promises to His people.

Amazingly, there's even more evidence. John chapter 6 is filled with verses that assure Christians of their eternal salvation. Jesus says in John 6:37, "All that the Father gives me will come to me. And whoever comes to me, I will never cast out." Jesus is saying no one can come to Him unless the Father draws that person, and all that the Father draws will certainly come. For everybody who does come, who certainly will come, Jesus will never cast them out. But notice how He goes on in verses 39 and 40, and He says, "And this is the will of Him who sent me that I should lose nothing of all that He has given me, but raise it up on the last day. For this is the will of my Father that everyone who looks on the Son and believes in Him should have eternal life, and I will raise Him up on the last day."

Notice how absolutely affirming those verses are about the security of our salvation. Jesus is saying this is God's will, and we know the Bible says God's will will be done. Psalm 115:3, "Our God is in the heavens. He does all that He pleases." He will have His way. Jesus is revealing to us here that the will of the Father is for Jesus to lose nothing of all that the Father gives Him. Since the Father gives the Son a people, He will lose none of those people. Not only that, He says that it's the will of God that everyone who looks to Jesus for salvation will have eternal life, and Jesus will *absolutely* raise them up on the last day.

So again, notice the absolute guarantee of this. If you are a Christian, it means that you have been drawn by the Father to Jesus. You came because the Father was drawing you, and the promise you have is that Jesus will never cast you out. He will never lose you, and He most certainly, absolutely, 100% will raise you up on the last day. Something else to think about here is that if Jesus loses even one of His people, then He has failed in His mission and to do the will of God. But, praise the Lord, Jesus never fails to do the will of the Father.

Another passage related to this topic is found in Romans chapter 8. There, we find the golden chain of salvation. In Romans chapter 8, beginning in verse 29 and continuing to verse 30, we read, "For those whom He foreknew, He also predestined to be conformed to the image of His Son, in order that He might be the firstborn among many brothers. And those whom He predestined, He also called. And those whom He called, He also justified. And those whom He justified, He also glorified." Now notice the continuation there from one to the other, but right there at the end, it's incredibly important because He says those whom He has justified, pause for a second, every person who's a believer in Christ has been justified. It means that we have been declared righteous in the eyes of

God, not because we are righteous, but because the righteousness of Christ has been imputed to us through faith.

If you're a Christian, you've been justified, and the Bible says those whom He justified, He also glorified. But hold on a second; we know that glorification doesn't come until glory, until Jesus returns, and we have the resurrected bodies and enter into that eternal, glorious state. How can the Bible say that we have already been glorified when we haven't? Well, here's what's happening. Our future glorification is so certain and guaranteed in the mind of God that it can be said that we have it now. That's how guaranteed and certain it is that God can even say right now that glorification is ours because it is guaranteed to happen.

The other important point on this that I want you to understand is that we remain Christians not because of how great we are or how faithful we are but because of how great God is. We remain Christians because of God. The Bible says in 1 Peter 1:5 that "we are kept by the power of God for this salvation that's going to be revealed in the last day." So, notice God is the one who is keeping us. We are not keeping ourselves Christians; He is keeping us in the faith. We also know that John 10:28 says that "no one can snatch [us] out of [Jesus'] hand." Well, if no one can snatch us away from God's hands, we certainly can't pull ourselves away from God's hands.
He keeps us and protects us, so our salvation is secured not because of us but because of
God.

It reminds me of when my oldest son was just over a year old. I would hold him all the time, and occasionally, we would be running or jumping or doing stuff while I was holding him, and he would get scared that he was going to fall, so he would grip onto me with a death grip, as much as a one-year-old has a death grip. He would cling to me with everything he had, and he believed that he was secure and safe from falling away because of how much he was grabbing me and how tightly he was holding onto me. In reality, though, he was safe and secure because he was holding onto me; I was holding onto him, and I was not going to let anything happen to him. He was secure because I was holding him, not because he was holding me. Well, the same thing applies to us and God. We are secure in our salvation and can trust that we will never lose it *not* because of how tightly we hold onto it, *not* because of how faithful we are, but because God holds onto us. He keeps us and keeps us from falling away.

So what about Christians who backslide? Is it possible for Christians to backslide and wander away? Yes, absolutely. That happens from time to time, but they will always come back. True Christians will never walk away for good. However, that raises one final question: "What about those who claim to have been Christians for a time and then deconvert?" You know, we live in the deconstruction age where people are talking about deconstructing and deconverting, and there is this almost glamor behind it right now. What about those people? They claim to have believed in Jesus and were Christians for a while, but they walked away, and now they are no longer Christians. What do we say about them?

Now, I don't want just to offer my opinion, but biblically speaking, the Bible would say that those people were never actually truly Christians in the first place. They might have had a lot of spiritual experiences. They might have had a lot of religious experiences. They might have had a lot of meaningful experiences. They could have participated in the work of God. They could have engaged in missions, efforts, and activities. But when it comes down to it, the Bible would say that they were never actually truly Christians.

In fact, in 1 John, John talks about people who had gone out of the church. They had been in the midst of the church. They were among the church. They were active in the church, and he says in 1 John 2:19, "They went out from us, but they were not of us; for if they had been of us, they would have continued with us. But they went out that it might become plain that they all are not of us." So the Bible says it's absolutely possible that there are going to be people who will give Christianity a try, and they will even convince themselves that they are true Christians, but one day they will fall away, and it's because they've never actually truly been born again. They've never truly been converted. They haven't truly repented of their sins and given themselves to Jesus. One of the surest signs of true faith is perseverance in the faith. If we are of Christ, we will continue with Christ.

And so the good news here is that if you are a true Christian, you cannot lose your salvation, and praise God for that. It is secure, and you will always remain safe in the arms of God because He holds onto you. So I hope that encourages you to know that you can't lose your salvation and that you are secure in your salvation not because you're great or because you're super faithful, but because God keeps you and you can trust Him.

Chapter 7

Are Christians Supposed to Speak in Tongues?

✝

I want to start this off by providing a simple answer: no. If you're asking are Christians supposed to speak in tongues, meaning every Christian *must* do this, the answer is an emphatic no. I need to say at the start that there is a lot of confusion about this today, and there are a lot of ways to trouble people and confuse people.

For instance, I remember I had been a Christian for only a couple of months, and I was at my uncle's funeral when I was approached by a woman who was a professing Christian, a woman that I knew to be a Christian and had a level of respect for. She approached me and said, "Hey, I heard you're a Christian now." I replied by saying, "Yes, ma'am, the Lord saved me. It's amazing, you know. I'm still trying to figure out what being a Jesus follower means, but life is great." But then she asked me: "Well, have you spoken in tongues yet?" I, of course, said, "No." Again, I had only been a Christian for a couple of months. I didn't even really know what that meant. And she said, "Oh, well, I'm sorry to tell you, but you're not actually a Christian." I was so confused. I knew I had repented of my sins, I had believed in Jesus and what He had done for me, and I had put all my faith and trust in Him, but now, here she was saying that even though I had done all of that, I wasn't actually a Christian because I hadn't spoken in tongues.

That experience really messed me up for a little bit. I mean, it really confused me. So I had to do a lot of research of my own and a lot of searching. I'm concerned that there's that same perception still out there today that if you don't speak in tongues, then you're not actually a Christian. That's why this question is important.

So, let's get into what the Bible actually says about this. One of the most important passages, arguably the most important passage, in the New Testament about speaking in tongues is found in Acts chapter 2, beginning in verse 1, which says,

> When the day of Pentecost arrived, they were all together in one place. And suddenly there came from heaven a sound like a mighty rushing wind, and it filled the entire house where they were sitting. And divided tongues of fire appeared to them and rested on each one of them. And they were all filled with the Holy Spirit and began to speak in other tongues as the Spirit gave them utterance. Now there were dwelling in Jerusalem Jews, devout men from every nation under heaven. And at the sound of the multitude came together and they were bewildered because each one was hearing them speak in his own language. And they were amazed and astonished, saying, "are not all of these who are speaking Galileans?" And how is it that we hear each of us in his own native language?... both Jews and proselytes, Cretans, Arabians, we hear them telling in our own tongue the mighty works of God.

Now, that's an incredibly important passage for a number of reasons, but basically, what happens is Jesus had just ascended back into heaven, and so He told the disciples to wait until the Spirit came. They're gathered together in one place, waiting for the Spirit to come. This is an act of obedience to the Lord's command, and then the Spirit does descend upon them. They see these divided tongues, and there's fire, which, in the Bible, is normally a symbol of the presence of the Lord. Then, they began to speak in other tongues. The most important thing you need to note here is that the word "tongues" simply means languages. A tongue was just another language. It was a known language.[5]

This means the disciples, even though most of them were Judeans and Galileans, were speaking in all these other languages from every nation under the sun, even though they didn't know those languages. The Spirit had given them the ability to communicate in these other known languages. Verse 11 is incredibly important because notice that it says, "We hear them telling in our own tongue." So, people who didn't know the language were speaking the language. It says, "telling in our own tongues the mighty works of God." In other words, the disciples weren't just speaking in these other languages as a show, act, or sign that they were filled with the Spirit. *It was not an end in and of itself.* It was a *means*. The purpose of these tongues was to communicate the Word of God. It was to communicate the Gospel of God and tell people about the mighty works of God. Don't miss that: **the purpose of these tongues was to tell people about God in a language that the one speaking didn't know so that others who did know that language could hear about God in their own language.** To make it very clear, speaking in tongues was the ability to speak in a language you didn't know to communicate the Word of God.

There's some really cool biblical theology going on here in Acts chapter 2 as well because Acts chapter 2 is actually the undoing of Babel. If you remember Genesis chapter 11, the Great Tower of Babel, think back to what happened. There was the flood, and then after the flood, God made a covenant with Noah and his family, and then we got the Table of Nations and read about all of Noah's descendants. The context of those chapters makes it clear that the people were supposed to continue on fulfilling the purpose that God had given Adam and Eve. Remember, God told Adam and Eve they were to be fruitful and multiply and fill the earth and have dominion over it (Genesis 1:28). So all the people who came from Noah were supposed to spread out. They're supposed to go across the world, have dominion over the world, and fulfill God's original purpose.

But what do they do instead? They're united together. They're all in one place, and it's an act of *disobedience*. God said, "Go," but they said, "Actually, we're going to stay." So they stayed and gathered together in one place. Not only that, but they were unified in an act of disobedience with sinful intentions. They said, "Let us make a name for ourselves." They wanted to be great. They essentially said, "We're going to build this tower. It's going to go all the way up to heaven."

Basically, the idea was they thought that they could dethrone God. They thought they were actually going to make it to the throne room of God. They were going to kick Him off the throne. They were going to be gods, but then the Lord looked down on them and said, "Hey, what are they even doing? We've got to get out of heaven and literally come down to the earth even to see what's going on down there." So God descends upon the earth and sees that they are united in this act of sinful disobedience. What does He do? He wants to put an end to their sinful purposes, so He confuses their languages. They're no longer able to understand each other.

So it's ironic, right? There are people who are literally from the same family and from the same place, but they can't understand what each other is saying because their languages have been confused. Finally, God actually scatters them and sends them on their way.

Now look at Acts chapter 2. It's the undoing of Babel because we see that the people are in one place just as they were in Genesis 11, but this time, it's an act of *obedience* because remember Jesus said, stay here, wait for the Spirit. So there they are waiting for the Spirit, and the Spirit comes and gives them the ability to communicate with people that they don't know and from places they've never been, and they're actually able to talk with them. So it's literally the reverse of Babel. This is a great example of how Jesus fulfills all the promises of God and undoes sin's curse. He continues to undo sin's curse by the giving of the Spirit, who undoes the curse of Babel and allows people to understand each other in languages they don't even know. This is a crucial point to understand with Acts chapter 2, that it's a continuation of redemptive history unfolding before us and showing how Jesus is righting all of our wrongs, especially through the giving of the Spirit.

One final note I want to make on this point is that almost all modern tongues are completely 100% unbiblical. Now, that might sound incredibly emphatic, and like maybe I'm overstepping there, but just think about a couple of the examples that we see in modern tongues today. When you hear about people speaking in tongues or think about people speaking in tongues, you're normally thinking about some sort of utterance that makes no sense, right? This is especially prominent in the Charismatic Church. Whenever they speak in tongues, it's in this unintelligible babbling; these utterances are just gibberish, and no one can understand it, but they pass it off as speaking in tongues.

Here's what we're going to say about this. Regardless of how they feel, and again, we want to be cautious of people's feelings, but at the end of the day, the Word of God is truth, and so regardless of what they say and how they feel, we go back to the Word of God for our answers. The Bible says that tongues were *known languages*. They were not babblings, they were not gibberish, and they were not utterances that nobody had the ability to understand. Speaking in tongues was the ability to communicate the Word of God in a language you didn't know for the purpose of telling people who spoke that language about the wonderful works of God.

What would this look like today if this gift still exists? Imagine a person is visiting somewhere like Brazil. He has never been to Brazil and doesn't know Portuguese at all, but he wants to witness to some people while in Brazil, and the person is trying his best to communicate with the locals. All of a sudden, he starts preaching the gospel and telling people about Jesus and how you can know him as your Lord and Savior, and come to find out, he was actually preaching in Portuguese the entire time. He didn't realize that he was doing it. He didn't know Portuguese, but the Spirit had given him the ability to communicate the Word of God and the mighty works of God, especially the gospel of God, in a language he didn't know. That would be an example of what a modern-day speaking in tongues would look like. But this rolling around on the floor, speaking in gibberish and utterances and things like that, is not biblical tongues. That is very easily disproved.

So again, I just want to encourage you by telling you that you do not have to speak in tongues to be a Christian. In fact, the Bible makes it very clear that the gift of tongues is not given to every single Christian (1 Corinthians 12:10, 30). According to the Bible, in order to be a Christian, you must repent and believe. If you have turned from your sins and you've trusted in Christ alone for your salvation, then you are right in the eyes of God through faith in what Jesus has done for you. You are justified by grace through faith. That's all you need for salvation. Speaking in tongues is not a requirement for salvation, so look to Jesus, not to tongues.

Chapter 8

Who Was St. Patrick?

✝

I think most people know about St. Patrick's Day, or at least they know how we celebrate it and when we celebrate it here in the United States. But you might not be as familiar with who Patrick actually was. For instance, his name wasn't actually Patrick. At his ordination, he was given the name Patrick, but his birth name was the Celtic name Maewyn Succat.[6] Another interesting fact is he wasn't actually Irish. He was British. He grew up in Britain. Born in the year AD 387 and died in AD 461, Patrick came from a fairly religious family, but it does seem, based on historical records, that the religion of his family was more of a cultural Christianity, what we would call nominal Christianity today, rather than a true commitment to Christ.[7]

Patrick's early years were interesting. When he was a teenager, some Celtic pirates from Ireland came and invaded his hometown, ransacking, pillaging, and capturing people. While Patrick's family was able to escape, he was not. Patrick was kidnapped and taken away. He was then sold as a slave, and during his enslavement, he was almost always isolated and alone. One of his main responsibilities as a slave was serving as a shepherd, which meant that he was in total isolation at that point.[8]

So, what do you do when you're enslaved and you're suffering from freezing cold temperatures and isolation and hunger? Well, Patrick prayed. He prayed hundreds of times a day, almost keeping in constant communion with God in prayer on a daily basis. Patrick, reflecting on this time in his life, wrote, "The Lord opened up my awareness of my lack of faith. Even though it came about late, I recognized my failings. So I turned with all my heart to the Lord my God. And he looked down on my lowliness and had mercy on my youthful ignorance. He guarded me before I knew him and before I came to wisdom and could distinguish between good and evil. He protected me and consoled me as a father does for his son."[9] God used this time in Patrick's life to teach him to be content with God alone, to teach him that even if he was alone and isolated and no matter what he was going through, no matter how hard it was, that the presence of the Lord was with him and the Lord was teaching him to be content with His presence alone.

Six years after he was initially enslaved, Patrick escaped and could board a ship and return home. Now, many might assume that having been kidnapped and enslaved and only barely able to escape, Patrick would've been content to stay in his homeland forever, and he might have done that, except he began to have visions. One night, as he was beginning to fall asleep, Patrick had a vision, and in the vision, he saw an Irishman holding up countless letters. One of them was titled "The Voice of the Irish." As Patrick saw these words, he heard the cries of countless people. They were the cries of the Irish people begging him to come back and walk among them again.[10]

Patrick was conflicted because he was now a Christian and wanted to be faithful to the Lord and His calling, but Patrick associated Ireland with pain, torture, enslavement, and isolation. He really did not want to go back there because he had such bad memories of being there. He ignored the vision initially and decided not to do anything, but the Lord was persistent. Patrick kept having vision after vision after vision, and it was the same one over and over and over and over again until finally Patrick responded and said, "If this is from you, Lord, I'm willing to go."[11]

Interestingly, though, he didn't immediately go back to Ireland. Most historians believe that Patrick spent the next two decades preparing for that return. During that time, he underwent much theological, ecclesiastical, and spiritual training so that when he did finally return to Ireland, he would be equipped to reach the Irish people with the gospel.[12] After that 20-year period, when Patrick was 48 years old, he was ordained into the priesthood. He was officially commissioned and sent out as one of the very first church planters to reach an unreached group, the Celtic people of Ireland.

Think about how encouraging this is. Almost everybody today knows the name St. Patrick, and they definitely know about St. Patrick's Day. He was 48 years old when he finally went back to Ireland. Let that be an encouragement to you who might be tempted to think that you're too old to do something great for God. That is never the case. If you are still alive today, God can use you to do great things in this world. You might be thinking that your prime is behind you, but God might have something great in front of you.

So Patrick was 48 years old when he was ordained, given the name Patrick, and sent out to go reach the Celtic people of Ireland. We can also learn a lot about his methods when he returns to Ireland. Because, at the time, the Celtic people of Ireland were barbarians and they were a rough group of people. They had a very pagan culture. And yet, Patrick never dismissed the Celtic culture. Rather, he engaged it. He connected with the people. He spent time with the people to get to know them and find out their needs so that he could show them how God could meet their needs. That's not to say that his mission was always easy; it wasn't. Patrick himself even records that from the moment of his arrival, he was almost continually placed in life-and-death situations, and the Celtic people were constantly threatening to torture him and kill him.[13]

However, Patrick continued to trust God. He continued to identify with the Irish people and use their cultural and religious understandings to lead into conversations about the one true God and minister to them in love and patience. What ended up happening is that God blessed Patrick's ministry greatly. There ended up being mass conversion in Ireland. Because of Patrick's specific approach of engaging with the people, getting to know the people, embracing their culture, using it to lead into gospel conversations, using their culture to point out their need for God, loving people, and being patient with them, to this day, Ireland is still the only country that has ever experienced mass conversion to Christianity without any bloodshed.[14]

Patrick modeled love and then was able to tell people about the source of that love. Therefore, remember the true story when you think about St. Patrick's Day. It's a shame that St. Patrick's Day is celebrated by wearing green, hanging shamrocks everywhere, and pinching people. For many people, it's a drinking holiday. In reality, St. Patrick's Day should be a day where Christians celebrate the mass conversion that took place in Ireland by God working through a humble, willing servant like Patrick.

So, next St. Patrick's Day, take time to celebrate God's work in the life of Patrick. Take time to thank God for the mass conversion that took place in Ireland. Take time to thank God for using ordinary, everyday people, even people with a troubled past, like Patrick, to accomplish great things. Then, look at your own life and ministry and seek to imitate Patrick's ministry. When thinking about how to engage with the world and the culture around you, think about what Patrick did. Embrace people where they're at. Meet them where they are. Use the culture to lead into gospel conversations. Be patient with people. Love people. And trust God always. When we wonder, "Who was St. Patrick?" that's who he was. He was a man who was saved by the grace of God in Christ Jesus, who was convicted and called by God to reach the people he associated with pain, torture, and enslavement, and he took the gospel to them. And by God's grace, there was mass conversion. Take time to praise the Lord, for He is worthy.

Chapter 9

Who Decided Which Books of the Bible to Include and Exclude?

✝

That is a very good question because it has so many misconceptions today, doesn't it?

If you ask people this question, there are all sorts of misconceptions. In fact, you'll often even see secular publications that'll post articles and print magazines that give their two cents about how it actually happened, and almost none of them take into account the actual history, which is unfortunate.

First, let's address a few misconceptions. One of the most common ones is that a certain council sat down together and had all these different books before them, and they sorted through them all and basically just picked and chose their favorites. Many think that's how they decided which ones were going to make it in. They sat down as a council, and they just made a decision as an authoritative body.[15] However, that never happened.

Another popular idea is that a pope issued a decree giving an official statement about which books to include and exclude. Along these same lines, others think that an emperor decided that he would take it upon himself to say which books of the Bible were to be included and excluded based on his personal preferences and which ones he liked.[16] These misconceptions are also popular in media, such as The Da Vinci Code, right? If you have read that book or possibly seen the movie, you know that the author, Dan Brown, says that Emperor Constantine is the one who actually decided which books of the Bible were supposed to be included and which ones were supposed to be excluded. Unfortunately, what happens is people either read that book or see that movie, and they think that must be what actually happened. So they start entertaining all of these ideas that aren't founded or based on history at all. So, there are a lot of misconceptions and a lot of confusion on this topic. To put it plainly, though, no council, pope, or emperor was responsible for picking and choosing the books of the Bible.

So, let's get into what actually happened. Almost all of the New Testament authors were Apostles. I say almost all because we don't know who wrote Hebrews. It could have been Paul, could have been Luke, could have been someone else; we don't know. God will let us know when we get to glory. Since almost all of the New Testament authors were Apostles, they wrote with God-given authority and inspiration. The word inspiration means breathed out by God, which comes from 2 Timothy 3:16. After the authors finished their writings, they would send them to the churches, and then the churches would receive those writings as authoritative or canonical.

You'll often hear people talk about the canon of the Bible, and the word canon simply means rule or standard.[17] The word of God is our standard. It is our rule for our lives. After the churches received the writings, they recognized them as authoritative and canonical and began to teach and preach from them in their gatherings. Even the Apostles themselves recognized each other's writings as authoritative and from God. In other words, when the Apostles read each other's writings, they considered each other's writings to be Scripture. We see this very clearly in 2 Peter 3:16, where Peter refers to the writings of Paul as Scripture.[18] Even though they were contemporaries of each other, writing at the same time, they immediately recognized that what they were doing was writing Scripture.

By the end of the Apostolic Period, the churches had already started to copy the books of the New Testament and send them around to other churches. They collected them alongside the Old Testament as the standard for God's people. They recognized the Old Testament as being Scripture and were starting to do that as early as the Apostolic Period with the Apostles' writings in the New Testament.[19] The Apostles' disciples would then use the Apostles' writings to teach and preach in the churches. Then, the disciples of the Apostles had disciples themselves, which resulted in a long line of people coming from the Apostolic teaching and authority, and they could recognize the Apostolic authenticity and authority.[20]

So think about it like this: because the people who were teaching and preaching, collecting, copying, and distributing were either the disciples of the Apostles or the direct successors of the disciples of the Apostles, they had a unique perspective to be able to tell which books actually came from the God-inspired Apostles. They would be able to recognize, yes, this is clearly from Paul. This is clearly from John. This is clearly someone who has been inspired of God. Then, they would hold those writings to be authoritative and use them to teach and preach in the churches. Therefore, as long as they knew that the books they had came from one of the

God-inspired Apostles, those books functioned as Scripture in the church.

However, it's true that there were many false writings as well. Sometimes, people would present a written work and attribute it to an Apostle or a disciple of Jesus. They would put the name of a disciple or a follower of Jesus on that writing in order to try to pass it off as Scripture. We know of a few of these, like the Gospel of Thomas, the Gospel of Mary, the Gospel of Judas, and plenty more to go around. But all of these were revealed to be forgeries and deceptively attributed to God-inspired Apostolic authors. Furthermore, and most importantly, none of these false gospels were ever universally received or accepted by the church.[21] So Christians don't deny that forgeries existed. However, the historical record testifies to the fact that they were never universally received or accepted by the church, and they were quickly shown to be forgeries and false writings.

We also know that some books that we have in our New Testament today were doubted at some point. We know, for instance, books like Hebrews, James, 2 Peter, 2 and 3 John, Jude, and Revelation were all doubted at some point.[22] People weren't immediately sure whether or not these were Apostolic writings that should be used as Scripture. However, the doubts and the exclusion of these books were also *never universal* in the church. By the fourth century, the doubts and possible exclusions ceased. In fact, by the end of the Patristic Period, referring to the period of the early church fathers, all churches worldwide shared the same New Testament canon with the same 27 books that we have in our New Testament today.[23] That's encouraging for everybody who wants to say that the canon wasn't decided until much later, that there's still doubt, and that people were picking and choosing. No, by the end of the Patristic Period, they had the exact same New Testament with all the same books that we have today.

To summarize this discussion, when it comes to the canon of Scripture and trying to understand why certain books were included while others were excluded, we need to understand today that no pope ever decided which books to include or exclude. No emperor, not even Constantine, sorted through various books, deciding which ones to include and which ones to exclude. No council, not even the council of Nicaea, ever sat down and just put all the possible books on the table and said, "All right, guys, let's go through these, figure out which ones we like, which ones we don't like, which ones we're going to use, and which ones we're not going to use."[24]

It is true that certain councils published lists of the official canon, but those lists were simply an *affirmation* of the canon, not a *prescription* of the canon. In other words, they were not *prescribing* the list because they, in their own authority, had decided the canon. They were sitting down saying, "Okay, these are the books that all the churches around the world have agreed are inspired of God, come from an Apostolic writer, and have been recognized to have Apostolic authority and inspiration behind them. These are the ones that are being used to teach and preach in the churches, so we are affirming the canon that the churches have already been using since the Apostolic period. We are just announcing that this is an affirmation that, yes, this is the canon." But they weren't pre-scribing, saying, "Based on our authority, we are putting this forward as our verdict about what we think the canon should be." It was an organic, Spirit-led process from the start.

So don't believe any of these myths about a single person or even a group of people sitting down and trying to decide which ones to include or which ones to exclude. God inspired authors to write the New Testament, and the churches, once they received those writings, received them as authoritative and started teaching from them and preaching from them. Even the other apostles who were writing Scripture recognized the other writings of the Apostles as scripture. This was the organic process that took place, and God oversaw the whole thing from the start. So, we can be very confident that the books in our New Testament are the only ones that should be included in the New Testament.

Chapter 10

Are the Jews Still God's Chosen People Today?

✝

One of the reasons this question is so interesting is because I always want to know what people mean by that. We use that terminology, *people of God*, all the time, especially in relation to this question, but what does that mean? Oftentimes, when people use this phrase of the Jewish people, they almost seem to believe that every Jewish person who has ever lived and will ever live will be saved as if by being Jewish, they get an automatic ticket to heaven. However, biblically speaking, that's just not the case. It's interesting that Christians would believe that considering the fact that the Bible teaches that the only people who will be saved are those who repent and believe, who put all their trust in Jesus alone. There is no salvation outside of Christ. So, there's no biblical reason to believe that any person or group of people, even the Jews, will be saved apart from repentance and faith in Christ.

So what does it actually mean, this phrase, *people of God*? What did it mean initially when it was first used regarding Israel? Interestingly, after God delivers the people of Israel out of Egypt, we read in Exodus 19:5-6, "Now therefore, if you will indeed obey my voice and keep my covenant, you shall be my treasured possession among all the peoples. For all the earth is mine, and you shall be a kingdom of priests and a holy nation to me." Now, notice that within the old covenant context, Israel's privilege as the people of God was conditional. *If* they obeyed and *if* they kept the covenant, *then* they would be God's covenant people out of all the people on earth.

Also, notice that this privilege of being the people of God came with a purpose. They were to be a kingdom of priests and a holy nation, which means essentially that Israel was meant to take the message of Yahweh to the surrounding nations. They were to be a light to the nations. You can read about that in Isaiah chapter 49 when God calls on Israel as His servant to serve as a light to the Gentiles to the nations. They were to tell the nations about Yahweh, the one true God, and exhort people to turn from their sins and put their faith in God. Therefore, as God's chosen people, Israel was to remain faithful to the covenant. *If* they were faithful and *if* they served as a light to the Gentiles, *then* they would be God's treasured possession, His people.

Well, here's the problem: Israel failed to be what God called them to be, and they failed to do what God called them to do. They failed as the people of God. They were consistently disobedient and unfaithful to the Lord and to His covenant. When that happened, as we read all throughout the Old Testament, the Lord brought judgment upon them. He brought the curses of the covenant upon them. This cycle repeated throughout all of Israel's history.

Not only that, but the people of Israel also failed to be the light to the nations and the kingdom of priests that they were called to be. God said they were to go to the nations, to be a light to the nations, but in most of the Old Testament, Israel just stayed in their own place and never went to the nations. If you read the Old Testament, it seems like the only kind of missionary story we read about is when Jonah begrudgingly goes to Nineveh to preach. Of course, it's begrudgingly because he didn't want to go, and God had to send a giant fish to swallow him and take him to Nineveh. That seems to be the only time that we even read about some sort of missionary activity on the part of the people of Israel to go and reach the pagan nations. So, by the end of the Old Testament, the people of Israel had failed as the people of God.

Then starts the New Testament, and here comes Jesus. Jesus comes on the scene, and He succeeds everywhere that humanity and Israel failed. He was faithful in all the places that we and Israel were unfaithful. What's really cool is if you just read the first four chapters of the book of Matthew, you will literally see Jesus reliving Israel's history and being faithful and obedient everywhere that they failed.

If you open up to Matthew and look at the first four chapters, you'll see things like the fact that Israel was called the Son of God, and they were called out of Egypt (Exodus 4:22, 12:33-42). Well, Matthew tells us that Jesus was called the Son of God, and God called Jesus out of Egypt (Matthew 2:13-15). We see an evil ruler who sought to eliminate the people of Israel and their deliverer by killing all male children two years old and younger (Exodus 1:8-22). Likewise, we read in Matthew that an evil ruler sought to eliminate Jesus by killing all two-year-old and younger male children (Matthew 2:16-18). After leaving Egypt, the people of Israel passed through the waters of the Red Sea, after which time God proclaimed them to be His treasured possession (Exodus 14, 19:5-6). Well, we read in the New Testament after Jesus left Egypt, He passed through the waters of the Jordan in baptism, after which time God proclaimed Him to be His beloved son (Matthew 3:13-17). After passing through the waters, Israel wandered about in the wilderness for 40 years, constantly giving into the temptations of the devil (Numbers 32:13). After Jesus passed through the waters, He wandered in the wilderness alone for 40 days, withstanding temptations from the devil (Matthew 4:1-11).

Very interestingly, after Jesus rebukes Satan and begins His public ministry, Matthew quotes the Old Testament to show how Jesus fulfills Israel's purpose, saying, "The people dwelling in darkness have seen a great light, and for those dwelling in the region and shadow of death, on them a light has dawned" (Matthew 4:15-16, quoting Isaiah 9:1-2). In other words, Jesus is the faithful, obedient Son that Israel was supposed to be, and He is the light of the world and the light to the world that Israel was supposed to be. So, the New Testament makes it very clear that Jesus is God's true Israel.

So, we begin to think about who the people of God are now. Who are the ones that God treasures, and who are the ones who are to serve as lights to the world? Well, it's the church. Another way of saying that is it's all people who have repented of their sins and trusted in Christ alone for salvation. Even another way to say that is it's all those who are *in Christ*. All who are in Christ are the people of God today. This is *not to say* that the church has replaced Israel; however, it is to say that the church has been grafted into the true Israel of God (Jesus), while those who reject Jesus as the Messiah (like the Jewish people do) have broken off from the true vine (Romans 11:17-24). Therefore, Christians have the distinct privilege, not through works of their own but completely through the grace of God in Christ, of being part of the true Israel of God.

There's great biblical support for this. Paul says in Romans 2:28-29, "For no one is a Jew who is merely one outwardly, nor is circumcision outward and physical, but a Jew is one inwardly, and circumcision is a matter of the heart, by the Spirit, not the letter." So Paul's saying you might have all the customs of the Jewish people, you might have the lineage, but being a Jew is not a matter of being one outwardly or any sort of traditional aspect, even circumcision; rather, it comes from the heart. It has to do with the heart, which is made clean and circumcised by the Spirit of God, which happens through repentance and faith in Christ.

Another example comes from Romans 9:6 and 8, "For not all who are descended from Israel belong to Israel. This means that it is not the children of the flesh who are the children of God, but the children of promise are counted as offspring." So again, Paul's saying you might have a Jewish lineage, but that does not mean that you are a child of God because it is not the children of the flesh who are the children of God, but it is the children of promise who are counted as offspring. Paul also says in Galatians 3:7, "Know then that it is those of faith who are the sons of Abraham." So, a Christian has more right to say that he is a son of Abraham than a Jewish person does who can trace his entire physical lineage back to Abraham because the true children of Abraham are those who have faith in Christ, according to the Bible. Galatians 3:29, "And if you are Christ's, then you are Abraham's offspring, heirs according to promise." So, he makes it even clearer. If you have rejected Jesus or do not believe in Jesus, then you are not a true offspring of Abraham. You are not a true child of Abraham, and so you cannot claim that for yourself. So, we see that Christians alone have this designation of being God's children and Abraham's offspring through faith in Christ.

Not only that but also the church takes up Israel's mission as well. Remember, they were to be a light to the nations, to take the knowledge of the Lord to the world who did not know him. Well, that's exactly what the Christian mission is today, right? Matthew 28, 18-20 is the Great Commission, where Jesus tells us to go and make disciples of all nations. In Ephesians 2:10,

God makes it clear that we have been saved for good works that He created for us beforehand. Matthew 5:14, Jesus literally calls his followers "the light of the world." Israel was to be a light to the nations. Jesus says of Christians, you are the light of the world. Let your light shine. 1 Peter 2:9 says, "Christians are a chosen race, a royal priesthood." Revelation 1:6 says that Christians are "a kingdom of priests." Basically, everything that is said of Israel in the Old Testament is said of the church in the New Testament. Therefore, Christians now have that designation of the children of God, the people of God, and we have all the same things said of us and attributed to us that were said of and attributed to Israel in the Old Testament.

So here comes an important question. Has God abandoned the Jews? Because there's a large group of Christians today who want to say yes, but the answer is no; God has not abandoned them at all. Now, they are considered as unbelievers. They are not believers because they reject Jesus as the Messiah and refuse to trust Him. Jesus even taught in the book of John that if God truly were your Father, then you would love Jesus (John 8:42). Well, Jewish people today want to say that God is their Father, that they believe in God, but the problem is they don't love Jesus. They've rejected Him. So, the Bible considers Jewish people today to be unbelievers, but God has not rejected them. That's Paul's whole point in Romans chapter 11. He says, of course, God hasn't abandoned Israel because look at me (Paul). He says I'm a Jew, and yet God saved me in Christ (Romans 11:1).

Furthermore, he informs us that there's always a remnant of those from Israel who will turn to faith in Christ (Romans 11:2-6), and it is the mission of the church today to take the gospel to the world, *including the Jewish people*, so that they might experience salvation in Christ. He goes on to say in Romans 11:26 that every Jewish person who will be saved will be saved in this way, through repentance and faith in Christ, after hearing the gospel message. There is no other way of salvation. Therefore, God has not rejected the Jewish people, turned His back on them, or replaced them; rather, He still reaches out to them through the missionary and evangelistic efforts of the church to lovingly call them to repentance and faith in Christ.

This is a big question, so let me just summarize a few points. First and foremost, the people of God are all those who are in Christ, no one else. Second, no person or group of people, including the Jews, will be saved apart from repentance and faith in Christ. It's impossible. So this idea is that just because they're Jewish and come from that heritage and lineage, God will give them a pass and a get-out-of-hell-free card, and they get to go to heaven simply because they come from a Jewish line, which is absolutely unbiblical. No person or group of people, including Jews, will be saved apart from repentance and faith in Christ. It's impossible. There is no salvation in any other name except the name of Jesus. Third, the church now has the same purpose as Israel did in being God's treasured people and serving as a light to the nations. Lastly, God hasn't abandoned the Jewish people. He has called Christians to go and reach them with the gospel.

Chapter 11

What Does the Bible Say About Psychics and Fortune Tellers?

✝

This is a good question to get into because I know these practices are prevalent in our culture today. So, we need to dig in and see what the Bible actually has to say about these things. First, we should note that the Bible strongly condemns things like mediums, the occult, and psychics. The Bible says in Deuteronomy 18:10-12, "There shall not be found among you anyone who burns his son or his daughter as an offering, anyone who practices divination or tells fortunes or interprets omens or a sorcerer or a charmer or a medium or a necromancer or one who inquires of the dead. For whoever does these things is an abomination to the Lord." These types of practices are explicitly condemned in Scripture. We need to understand that some common practices in our world today would fall into these categories. For instance, practices like horoscopes, tarot card readings, astrology, fortune telling, palm reading, and seances, the Bible condemns these things because they are demonic, pagan practices.

A question that goes along with this topic usually is, "Well, what about the accuracy?" Because some people might wonder, "How can psychics and fortune tellers be so accurate sometimes?" Many people have visited these types of people before and received some alarmingly accurate predictions. However, these practices have pretty much been debunked. Fortune tellers, mediums, and psychics have a number of methods to get accurate information from you. Many of them are just really, really good at deductive reasoning. They can make some accurate deductions based on appearances. They see the way you look, the way you dress, how you act, maybe who you came with, and they can deduce a lot of information from you in that way. Oftentimes, what they'll do is they'll ask you leading questions that are going to provoke answers and information from you. Unfortunately, we often end up giving away more information than we even intended to, so they take that information, rework it, and then use it later to seem like they have some supernatural insight.

Oftentimes, they'll have you book sessions ahead of time, and just based on your name and contact information, they can do a lot of research on you beforehand that they'll bring up at some point during the session and make it appear mystical. But at the end of the day, these are pretty much nothing more than parlor tricks that have been debunked. Oftentimes, fortune tellers and horoscopes, in particular, will say the most general bits of information, which could literally apply to anyone, but because we're already susceptible and we want to believe them, we think that they're giving us some great insight about ourselves. For example, you might read a horoscope that says, "If you're this sign or if you fall under this category, you're going to have a really stressful month full of setbacks." At the end of the month, you look back, and you're like, oh my goodness, I had a stressful month full of setbacks. Well, yeah, of course you did. We all did. We live in a stressful world, and almost every month, we have a certain level of setbacks, but it's just general information that gets put out there to make you believe that it is special or specific to yourself.

But a follow-up question asks, "Well, what about the times when they seem to give information that seems supernatural? What about the times when fortune tellers or psychics say things to us and tell us things that no one could possibly know?" I really hate to tell you this, but that is the result of demonic spirits. The Bible tells us in 2 Corinthians 11:14 that Satan and his demons masquerade as angels of light. So, of course, they would want to make you think that people participating in practices that are explicitly condemned in the Bible could offer you supernatural insight and information or even make you believe that you're talking to one of your deceased loved ones.

There's an example in Acts chapter 16 where there was a slave girl who seemingly had the ability to tell the future, and she made her owners a lot of money as a fortune teller. When Paul visited that area, he recognized immediately that this girl was possessed by a demon. The girl wouldn't stop pestering Paul, so he turned around and demanded that the demon come out of her. Once it did, she lost all of her supernatural abilities. That goes to show just how much these practices are connected with the demonic realm. So if you have sought out a medium or a psychic or attended a seance where someone claims to be communicating with your dead loved one and that dead loved one is talking to you and saying things to you, I'm really sorry to tell you this, but you have been deceived. That's the work of the demonic realm.

People might wonder why people seek out such things. If you just think about it, oftentimes, what they're wanting is insight. They want insight into themselves and into their life.

They think a horoscope can tell them why they are the way that they are. They think astrology can tell them why they are the way that they are. They think a psychic can tell them what will happen in their future or maybe whether or not a certain relationship is going to work out. Sometimes, they want closure, but at the end of the day, they seek some insight. However, all of these things are substitutes for God and the Bible. If you want to know why you are the way you are, you're going to find that answer in Scripture, and it will be very clear. It will provide you with more insight into yourself than anything else or anyone else possibly could. If you want to know what will happen in the future, you should turn to the one who is sovereign over the future. He might not give you all the details about what will happen, but at least you're going to be in a close relationship with the one who rules over all of the future, someone you can trust and depend on. You see, one of our biggest problems is that many times, we want to learn what's going to happen when God simply wants us to learn how to trust Him.

So, let's conclude with a number of takeaways. First and foremost, the Bible condemns all of these pagan practices. Second, they are heavily involved with and empowered by the demonic realm. Third, the dead cannot communicate with the living. Finally, remember that these things serve as sinful substitutes for God and the Bible. So, we should seek the one true God and dig into His Word.

Chapter 12

What Does it Actually Mean to be a Lukewarm Christian?

✝

If you'll indulge me for a moment, stop and think about how you would answer that question. If someone were to come along to you and ask you this question, "How can I know if I'm a lukewarm Christian?" how would you answer that question? As you answer, try to see how much of your answer is influenced by cultural understanding. If I had to guess, I think most people would answer that question by saying something like, "A lukewarm Christian is someone who is not on fire for the Lord, but it's someone who's also not cold toward the Lord either. This person believes in Jesus and attends church somewhat regularly, but he's not the most committed or devoted. He's just kind of lukewarm." But my question is this: is that what the Bible teaches about being lukewarm? I know that's the popular understanding and the popular way to answer that question, but we always have to ask ourselves, is that actually what the Bible teaches? So, we need to dive into the passage from which this phrase comes.

If you didn't know, this phrase actually comes from the book of Revelation. Revelation chapter three is the letter to the church in Laodicea. In verses 14-16, we read, "And to the angel of the church in Laodicea write: The words of the Amen, the faithful and true witness, the beginning of God's creation. I know your works: you were neither cold nor hot. Would that you were either cold or hot! So, because you are lukewarm and neither hot nor cold, I will spit you out of my mouth."

Now, let's just remember the context here. This is the book of Revelation. This is John, who is recording the vision that Jesus gave him to send to the seven churches in Asia Minor, one of which was the church in the city of Laodicea. A few facts about the city of Laodicea are essential for understanding the passage. First, they were a really rich city. They were actually pretty famous for the clothing that they made out of black wool. That's where a lot of their money actually came from.[25] They also had a leading medical school where they developed a special eye ointment.[26] So they had a lot going for them. However, the downside of Laodicea, the city, was that it didn't have its own natural water source. They had to bring in water from other cities through an aqueduct system. In those days, it was fairly common for cities to have aqueduct systems: one for hot water, which was used primarily for bathing and cleaning, and one for cold water, which was primarily used for drinking.[27]

Well, here's the kicker. As great as Laodicea seemed to be with all their money, fancy clothing, medical university, and eye salve, they were far away from all other cities. So by the time the water reached them, the hot water and the cold water were both, you guessed it, lukewarm. Also, since it had traveled such a long distance, it would pick up all kinds of minerals and bacteria. If you drank it without first boiling it, it would make you throw up. You would literally have to spit it out of your mouth.

So, think back to the passage. Knowing all of that background, think about how much of that cultural context Jesus references in this passage. He references both hot water and cold water. He references water so gross it makes people spit it out of their mouths, just as Jesus said that He was going to spit the church out of His mouth. Later on in the passage, Jesus even references the city's wealth. He references their clothing manufacturing and their eye salve. In other words, Jesus knows this city. He knows this church and is communicating to them in a way that will make sense to them. They would understand these references fully, even if today we have to do a little bit of research on them. But let's just get back to the water for a second. If hot water was good for bathing and cleaning and cold water was good for drinking, what was the lukewarm water good for? Nothing. It was useless water. We have to understand this cultural background in order to understand this passage because this passage gets absolutely abused today and totally misunderstood today.

You might hear it preached at a revival meeting or something like that, and they're going to say something like, "Jesus would rather you be cold toward Him than lukewarm toward Him. He would rather you reject Him entirely and be against Him than be one of these lukewarm Christians. He can stomach a cold person, but He can't stomach a lukewarm person." Listen, I know that'll preach for a lot of churches, but there are just a few problems with that message. First and foremost, does that align with anything else we read anywhere else in Scripture? There is nothing that I have seen in Scripture to suggest that Jesus would rather have people reject Him entirely than be indifferent toward Him. So, it doesn't align with the rest of scripture.

The other problem with this is that it totally misunderstands the point of the passage. It misses the entire message that Jesus is seeking to communicate to the church in Laodicea. The final problem is that we often read something into the text that's not there. The way this passage is typically preached is based entirely on modern cultural phrases. For instance, today, we'll say something's hot if it's really good, right? Think about basketball. If a basketball player hasn't missed a single shot all game, people say, oh, he's hot right now. He's got the hot hands right now. He's on fire. We do the same thing with Jesus. If someone's really passionate about Jesus and the gospel and the kingdom, they'll say that person is on fire for the Lord. Well, we do the same thing with cold today. We tend to associate cold with being bad. Again, if you're thinking about a basketball player, if someone is missing all their shots, you'd say they're cold right now, they're off. Or if someone is cold-hearted, that's an insult.

So, in our modern culture, hot means good, and cold means bad. But the problem is that no one in the ancient world would have thought like that. They didn't associate hot with good and cold with bad. That is a modern understanding that we have read back into the text, which is dangerous. That's called eisegesis when you read something into the text that's not there. We need to commit ourselves to exegesis, drawing out from the text what is there so that we can properly understand God's word. Did you happen to notice when we were reading the passage and when we did all that cultural context and background that both hot and cold water were good? Nothing in the passage said that hot water was good and cold water was bad. The background to the passage lets us know that hot water is good because we can use it to bathe and clean, and cold water is good because we can use it to drink and be refreshed. The only water that's not good is the lukewarm water, and it's not good because it can't be used for anything. It's useless.

And folks, that is the whole point of this passage. I wish people would understand that today, read it that way, and preach it that way. Here's a church that had the resources available to do great things for the kingdom of God, but instead, they were like their own sickening water: completely useless. So, to be a lukewarm Christian is to be a useless Christian. It's a person who either does nothing at all or who does the absolute bare minimum. They might attend a Sunday morning service, but that's about it. That's their entire faith. That is the only time they read the Bible. That is the only time they pray. That is the only time they have anything to do with God and His kingdom and His purposes at all. It's alarming how many people in the church that describes today. So, if that's what it means to be a lukewarm Christian, how can I tell if I am a lukewarm Christian?

Well, I would ask you a couple of questions. First and foremost, are you giving the bare minimum to the Lord? When you look at your life and think about what you're doing for God, His kingdom, and His purposes, are you giving the bare minimum? What are you doing for the kingdom of God? Not, are you doing something for the kingdom of God? My question is, what are you doing for the kingdom of God? Are you currently doing all that you can to demonstrate what life in God's kingdom is like to the world?

Because as Christians, as followers of Jesus, we're called to be imitators of Christ. We're called to reflect His nature and His character to the world. When you look at the Gospels, you see all that Jesus did, how He attended to the sick, to the hurting, to the depressed, to the broken hearted, to the poor, to the needy, to the hungry, to the thirsty, and you see how He cared for them, are you seeking to imitate that and demonstrate that in your life? If not, then you're not aligned with what it looks like to be part of God's kingdom. What are you good for? What's your use? What's your purpose? If you think about these questions and your answer time and time again is I am giving the bare minimum to the Lord, I'm not doing anything for the kingdom, I'm not serving a purpose right now, I'm not being useful for God and His kingdom, then, unfortunately, that would describe a lukewarm Christian. A lukewarm Christian is a useless Christian, and I hope that's not you. I hope that the cultural background of this passage has helped you understand it better and helped you see how important it is to do historical background when you're studying the Bible.

Chapter 13

Why Should We Believe in the Resurrection of Jesus? Featuring Pastor Jordan Massey

✝

The following transcript is of a conversation between Pastor Alex and the Associate Pastor of Georges Creek Baptist Church, Jordan Massey, as they seek to answer the question: Why should we believe in the resurrection of Jesus?

[Alex] I wanted to have Jordan on here because we end up almost every week at some point hanging out in each other's offices, talking about the sermons that we're writing and bouncing ideas off each other. And we thought, hey, man, it'd be a cool idea to record a podcast together, especially for

Easter, and talk about why we should believe in the resurrection of Jesus. And as Jordan and I were talking, we were thinking, well, there are a lot of different reasons, right?

[Jordan] Oh, yeah.

[Alex] Yeah, a lot of different reasons we should believe in the resurrection. But first and foremost, I think the main reason, and I think Jordan would agree with me, is that we should believe in the resurrection of Jesus because the Bible says Jesus rose from the grave. At the end of the day, that's what matters most, right? We have all these great pieces of evidence, and we are going to get into them in just a little bit, but at the end of the day, we need to believe something because the Bible says it. And the Bible says that after three days in the grave, Jesus rose from the dead. However, that does bring a little bit of a problem because, for instance, someone might say to you something like, well, I don't believe the Bible.

[Jordan] That's what you hear a lot of people say. They're like, well, that works out for you Christians because you believe the Bible, but what about me? I don't believe the Bible.

[Alex] Yeah. And so if you're witnessing to someone, that might be a common thing that they end up saying. And at the end of the day, your belief in the Bible is not what makes the Bible true. The veracity of the Bible is not conditioned upon your belief in it.

[Jordan] Yeah. And we always have to remember, too, as modern-day Christians, the Bible was here way before us. And unless Jesus comes back beforehand, the Bible is going to be here long after us, too. It's going to be just as true then as it's always been.

[Alex] Right. I've had this conversation with some people I used to work with. I told them I believe in the resurrection because the Bible says Jesus rose from the dead, and they said exactly what we're talking about. They said I'm not a Christian, so I don't believe in the Bible. And I said, well, you could also believe that you don't have to pay taxes. You might have that belief that, hey, I don't actually have to pay taxes. And that's okay. You're entitled to that belief, but come tax season, the IRS is not going to go, oh wait, hey, this guy, oh, he doesn't believe in paying taxes. So we're not going to do anything. That's fine. No, they're going to come after you. You're going to be audited, and they're going to get their money. So, just because you don't believe in something doesn't mean that it's not true. Or, for example, if you get pulled over for speeding, and you say, well, I don't believe I was speeding. And the cop says, well, I have you on radar, and you were, and you say, well, I don't believe I was, so you can't give me a ticket. The cop's going to look at you and say, okay, you can not believe it, but you're still getting the ticket because it's documented and proven. In other words, our belief in something, our acceptance of something, or even our adherence to something is not what makes that thing true. So people can choose not to believe in the Bible, but that in no way diminishes its truthfulness, reliability, or authority. The Bible is the inspired, inerrant, and fallible word of God. The Bible says in 1 Timothy 3:16 that Scripture is breathed out by God. And so if the Bible says it, it is true. And if it is true and it comes from God, that's all that we need for belief.

[Alex] But we understand that when you talk to others, they will want some other sort of evidence. And so Jordan was going to take on some of these.

[Jordan] Yeah. And right before we really jump into those pieces of evidence, I think, especially to tag off of what you were saying, Alex, about how important it is for us to understand what the Bible says is even to understand how important the Bible itself says the resurrection is. Because there are a lot of people out there who don't want to believe in miracles in the first place. Maybe they're okay with Jesus, but they're like, there's no way he rose from the dead. You silly Christians. But what the Bible says in 1 Corinthians chapter 15:17-19 is that "if Christ has not been raised, your faith is futile and you are still in your sins. Then those also who have fallen asleep in Christ have perished. If in Christ, we have hope in this life only, we are of all people most to be pitied."

[Alex] In other words, if Jesus is not alive today, all this is in vain.

[Jordan] Yeah. And all the people who've given their lives for it, it means nothing if Jesus didn't actually rise from the dead. So, this needs to be a topic that we, as Christians, take seriously. Yes. We celebrate it at Easter time, but we need to know why we believe it.

[Alex] Yeah. We need to know how foundational it is for our faith.

[Jordan] Yeah. Like you said, that does start with, for us, it starts with the Bible. We have to understand that the Bible says it is true. And if we claim to believe that the Bible is God's word, then we have to believe that it's true.

[Alex] Okay. So let me ask you this, then. The Bible also says that Jesus died on the cross. But there are people like atheists who deny that Jesus ever died. For instance, Muslims even believe that Allah spared Jesus from the cross, and there was someone substituted in his place. So, what do you do with that? What do you say to those people who would say, well, I don't know that I'm even convinced Jesus actually did die on the cross?

[Jordan] Yeah. It kind of plays into that swoon theory. What I grew up hearing it being called, right? That maybe Jesus just passed out on the cross. However, there are a good number of pieces of evidence for the fact that Jesus actually did die. And I want to lead off with what crucifixion actually was in the first place. The Romans created crucifixion as a mastery of the art of killing. It wasn't just torture. The torture was just the part of it. It's like the preamble to the final part there. This is terrifying, especially when we think of the things Jesus went through before He ever got to the cross. And then, when a person was on a cross, he would hang on that cross, and the goal was to make the victim suffocate. Because you're hanging there with your arms suspended, it's a fight to get every breath.

[Alex] Yeah. Your body weight is literally crushing your lungs at that point.

[Jordan] Yeah. And so for Jesus in particular, he has the nails most likely through the wrists. So every time He needs a breath at all, He has to pull up against the cross, against those nails, and also against the skin that was torn off of his back to get every single breath.

[Alex] And that wood, I mean, keep in mind, they weren't sanding it beforehand. So you've got rough wood and an open fleshed back with blood coming out.

[Jordan] Right. And He's up there for hours. And so then after Jesus died, which, by the way, there were eyewitness accounts of His last words right before He took his last breath. The eyewitnesses weren't just His followers. It was the Roman guard by the cross. Other people heard him say His last words and take His final breath. And then, after He died, they went to make sure. They took the spear, and they speared him into the side. And the purpose of that was to pierce the person's heart.

[Alex] Right.

[Jordan] And the Bible says that blood and water came out. A lot of modern scientists have pointed out that seems like pericardial effusion, which is where, at the point of or after the point of death, water or fluid starts to form around the heart. So, when it was pierced, most scientists believe it came out. Another scientific proof of death. But even after that, they would come and break their legs. This was another tactic that they used. Again, the purpose for the Romans was to kill the victims and to make sure that they died. If they took too long, then they would also go and break the legs of the victim.

[Alex] Because you can't lift yourself up at that point anymore.

[Jordan] Right.

[Alex] So you don't get any breath.

[Jordan] Yeah. But when they found Jesus, He was already dead. They proclaimed, hey, there's no need to break His legs because He's already dead. If they weren't sure, the Romans wouldn't have let Him go.

[Alex] Oh yeah, that's a good point. The Romans would have definitely been like, this is what we do in every other case. So we've got to break the legs. The only reason they would not have broken the legs is if He was already dead.

[Jordan] Exactly. And why would they want in any way to keep him alive? This is a man who, at least in their minds, is a direct threat to their own king.

[Alex] Yeah, that's right.

[Jordan] Someone that's being called the king of the Jews, they're not going to leave him alive.

[Alex] Right.

[Jordan] But that's even fulfilling a prophecy. Right?

[Alex] Not a bone would be broken (Numbers 9:12, showing Jesus as the true Passover Lamb).

[Jordan] That not a bone would be broken on Jesus. So they didn't even break his legs there on the cross. But the swoon theory says that He somehow survived all that and was just passed out, not dead.

[Alex] So even though He's already suffered. He's already been on the cross for hours. He's already, you know, had a spear through Him. All that kind of stuff. The Romans have pronounced Him dead. Everybody who's looking on knows that He has died at that point. There's even the Roman guard who says, surely we've just killed the son of God. Even though all of that has occurred, some believe He was just passed out.

[Jordan] Right. So then they're going to take this incredibly feeble and weak man, beaten, bruised, bloody, unrecognizably beaten man and put him in a tomb by himself, wrapped in burial cloths, and He's going to survive that?

[Alex] True. Good point.

[Jordan] He has no food, water, medicine, or one to take care of him inside that tomb.

[Alex] Right. So imagine you walk out on a busy interstate, get hit by a transfer truck, and roll under it. The next few cars come and get you to you. You bleed out on the highway, and somehow, your body rolls off onto an overpass or something. You're on the ground. Are you surviving without medical attention?

[Jordan] I would not think so.

[Alex] Probably not. We're not medical doctors, but I don't think you're surviving that. And yet, that's the claim. It's that maybe Jesus just suffered something equally horrendous but is still alive, and you put Him in a tomb without any medical attention whatsoever. And they're saying somehow He just happened to survive that and come out three days later.

[Jordan] Yeah. And that's, that's the difference between what people are trying to do. The swoon theory or what I call the swap theory with Islam. Most Muslims will tell you they hold Jesus in high regard. Right. And they're like, well, there's no way that God would allow Jesus to die.

[Alex] Yeah. They have a very high view of Jesus.

[Jordan] The thing is, though, that's exactly what Satan wants us to believe.

[Alex] Exactly.

[Jordan] Right. Because Satan didn't want Jesus to die either.

[Alex] Yeah. Just bow down to me. I'll give you all the kingdoms. I'll give you the crown without the cross.

[Jordan] Yeah. It's incredibly paramount for us that Jesus physically died.

[Alex] Absolutely.

[Jordan] Because that is our atonement. And so we can take what the Bible says about Jesus's death literally. We can look at the pieces of evidence that have been given, that have been shown from the Bible, from history, from science, even to show us that Jesus died on the cross.

[Alex] Okay. So He died on the cross. And part of the last kind of theory we were talking about is with this theory that, well, maybe he didn't actually die. We know that after three days, there was this giant stone that not a single person on their own could roll away.

[Jordan] Yeah.

[Alex] So they're thinking that someone who just suffered all of that and didn't receive any medical attention miraculously recovered after three days and rolled away that stone. Is that right?

[Jordan] Yeah. Well, the idea for that is ridiculous. And there are all kinds of theories, even to this day, of the stolen body that maybe the Jews stole the body, or some will even claim that the Romans themselves stole the body.

[Alex] Yeah.

[Jordan] This has always been a weird one to me because that would completely undo the entire purpose of killing Jesus for them in the first place. Right?

[Alex] Yeah. So this is something I like to look at with a detective's eyes. Growing up, I wanted to be Sherlock Holmes. I thought that was going to be my destiny. Never in a million years would have thought that I was going to be a pastor of a Baptist church, but God has a sense of humor. So when I think of the empty tomb, I think of a mystery because here are the facts. Okay. If you're just going to think about this very logically, think of it as a cool Sherlock Holmes mystery. The facts are that Jesus is dead and put in a tomb. And then that tomb is sealed with a ginormous stone that not a single person on their own could roll away. And then, outside of that tomb, there's an entire Roman guard. And we read about that in the Bible that they had placed Roman guards because they were like, Hey, there was all this stuff He said about how He's coming back and all this, you know, we're a little concerned. It could be true. And so Pilot's like, okay, you've got the green light, go stand outside the tomb, make sure you're stationed there. And so the facts are Jesus is dead. Jesus is in the tomb that is sealed with a huge stone, and there's a Roman guard outside of that tomb. And then, after three days, the facts state that the stone is rolled away and the tomb is empty. So my question is, where's the body?

[Jordan] Right.

[Alex] What happened there? And as you pointed out, one of the most common ones is when people say Rome stole the body. This is ridiculous because, as you just said earlier, that would defeat the purpose. Right?

[Jordan] Yeah.

[Alex] The reason that Rome wanted to kill Jesus is because Jesus was claiming to be the king of a kingdom. And that was a direct threat to Rome. And Pilot even asked Him, are you the king of the Jews? And Jesus is like, you say so. My kingdom is not of this world. They were threatened by His kingship. And so if you have a bunch of followers who have heard Jesus say, I'm going to die, but I'm going to come back. I'm going to rise from the dead. I'm coming back after three days. Then, as Rome, you steal the body after three days; what will the disciples think? Oh, Jesus is alive. We might not have gotten to see Him, but this is exactly what He said was going to happen.

[Jordan] Yeah. The Romans would do everything they could to convince everyone that Jesus was dead and He was going to stay dead.

[Alex] They were proclaiming victory in Christ's death. And so it would make no sense for Rome to steal the body because then that would start with the hysteria of these Jewish followers saying that Jesus is alive, that He actually did rise from the dead. And so naturally, people will go; if it wasn't Rome, then maybe it was the Jewish leaders. Literally, every suggestion for stealing the body falls on the same sword because the Jewish leaders might've had an in with Rome, you know, and the guards and everything. They possibly could have even gotten into the tomb if they wanted to. However, if they had stolen the body, you would have ended up with the same problem. It would have absolutely defeated their purposes. They steal the body. There's no Jesus. The disciples think He's risen. We didn't get to see Him, but we know that He's risen because he's not in there. And this is exactly what He said was going to happen.

[Jordan] Yeah. All the accounts show the religious leaders, the Jewish leaders, as the ones pushing for Jesus' death more than Rome was.

[Alex] Right.

[Jordan] They were the ones pulling all the strings, trying to get Jesus killed. Why? What would they have to gain from furthering a narrative that, hey, what if He's alive now?

[Alex] Yeah, exactly. So it makes no sense because they end up in this situation where they would want to preserve the dead body so that if anyone thought Jesus was alive, they could say, nope, come back to the tomb. I'll show you His body. He is dead. There's all your hope. And so I think kind of the last one that people entertain is maybe the disciples stole the body.

[Jordan] Right. Which is hilarious because the Bible even mentions that.

[Alex] Yeah. Right.

[Jordan] That the Jewish leaders are talking with the Roman guard, and they're like, Hey, what if we make up this story? Just in case.

[Alex] What if we make up this lie and just say that the disciples stole it? Right.

[Jordan] But my other favorite thing that makes that one ridiculous is, as you said before,
there is a Roman guard out there, and that doesn't mean one guard. That means a section
of soldiers that's out there guarding this tomb for this very purpose. And a bunch of fishermen and tax collectors are going to come to beat these fully armored soldiers and roll away the stone and get this body?

[Alex] The same people who, out of fear, deserted Him when He was being arrested in the first place.

[Jordan] Yeah.

[Alex] Those guys, you think those guys are now going to step up? They were afraid they were going to be crucified with Christ. You think after seeing Jesus be crucified, all of a sudden, they're emboldened to go and challenge Rome just to steal the body of Jesus. No, it doesn't happen that way. And the other thing that I think makes this ridiculous is if you look at the effect that His resurrection had on the early church and on those first disciples and those first followers of Christ, they go from these timid, scared followers to the most bold witnesses you can imagine and literally all 12 of Jesus's disciples apart from John end up dying a martyr's death and they're willing to. Peter denied Jesus three times because he was afraid that he was going to be crucified with Him when his time came, he said, do it upside down. I'm not even worthy to be crucified in the same way.

[Jordan] When I think of Peter, too, I think of his sermon at Pentecost, right? Peter went from, like you said, being so afraid of these leaders from Rome and the Jewish religious leaders that he denied Jesus three times, one of the times even calling a curse upon him because he was so afraid to be recognized as a friend of Jesus. And then, after seeing the resurrected Jesus, he's so emboldened by it that he preaches a sermon calling out those very religious leaders as the ones who killed Jesus.

[Alex] Yes, you did this. He's pointing the finger right at them. You just read the first couple chapters of Acts, and he's always going, you did this. This is on you. You messed up. You killed the anointed one of God.

[Jordan] Yeah. That doesn't seem like the same person who doesn't have a solid reason to make that change.

[Alex] Right. And so I think that's the point is if the disciples did steal the body, would
they have the type of courage that we read about in the gospels and in Acts in particular and in church history where we know that they go from being timid, fearful followers of Christ to all of them dying martyrs death?. And I just don't think if you made that up if you stole the body, you're not going to be willing to die for your lie. Not knowing it's a lie, many people will die for a lie. Hardly anyone will die for a lie, knowing that it's a lie.
So I think when you look at that as a detective, the empty tomb, and you're like, okay, what makes the most sense of the evidence that we're presented with? Let's follow the evidence to whatever conclusion it leads us to. And you look at the evidence and all of the facts surrounding the empty tomb, and you go away thinking, okay, I know this sounds crazy. I know it sounds impossible, but the best explanation of all of the given

data is that on the third day, Jesus Christ rose from the grave by the power of God.

[Jordan] Yeah.

[Alex] So Jesus did rise from the dead on the third day. And that was witnessed not just by those first disciples, but we know that Jesus had a number of resurrection appearances. And I think we're going to talk about this in a little bit, but what makes those so interesting is if he had only appeared to his own disciples, then that could be easily dismissed. But the resurrection appearances of Jesus occurred in a variety of places to a variety of people.

[Jordan] Exactly. History records, even outside of the Bible, even other historical sources from that time, there were over 500 eyewitnesses of a resurrected Jesus.

[Alex] Yeah. And what's interesting about that is, you know, sometimes I've heard people say when you bring up that He appeared to over 500 people at one time, people have tried to claim that was mass hysteria or delusion or some sort of like hallucination. And again, if you want to just look at modern science, if you look at psychology, it has been proven that there has never been a single instance of a joint hallucination or a mass hallucination of any kind. People typically will hallucinate what they anticipate seeing. So I've read it like this is that if a person is going through some sort of psychotic episode, they have all sorts of things that they anticipate that they're going to see, you know, it comes from paranoia, things like that. And so, they will have a hallucination based on what they think they're going to see or what they are afraid to see or expect to see. And again, besides that, there are no cases of mass hallucinations.

[Jordan] Right. And then the other thing about it is, as you said, it was also a variety of people. It wasn't just His apostles. It wasn't even just His followers. And we'll get to that in a second. But this is something I've heard a lot of apologists mention. I think it's really worth mentioning that the very first people who saw the risen Jesus and claimed to have seen the risen Jesus and took it back, and that is recorded in the Bible to have seen him, were women.

[Alex] That's right.

[Jordan] Right. And that was a big deal because, in that culture, women were not seen as a reliable source of information at that time.

[Alex] So if you're writing one of the Gospels, would you choose women to be the first people to discover the risen Jesus?

[Jordan] At that time? No.

[Alex] If you were making up a story and you were trying to convince someone, you would say, oh, Jesus was found by the high priest or by Pontius Pilate himself. You know, Caesar, Tiberius Caesar visited Jerusalem, and he was the first person to discover the empty tomb. You would go to some prominent figure who had some sort of respect in that society to be the one to find the empty tomb or be the first person Jesus appears to.

[Jordan] Yeah. I mean, it sounds like a more epic story for Jesus to like to appear first to Pilot. It would, but no, He shows up to a woman who was expecting him to be dead.

[Alex] Yeah.

[Jordan] He shows up to her, and she's the first eyewitness of the resurrected Jesus. There's no way these men would have written this account and taken it seriously in that way unless it was true.

[Alex] That's right. That's a great point.

[Jordan] But then it's not just the women; it's also other kinds of people. When you think about that, Jesus physically appeared to Saul of Tarsus, right? So this would take place a little bit later, right? Saul, at that time, was one of the greatest enemies of the followers of Jesus. I mean, he's literally traveling to a city to arrest followers of Jesus.

[Alex] This is after he had overseen the stoning of Stephen, by the way.

[Jordan] Right. Yeah. He was actively hunting down these Christians. He had already just executed Stephen.

[Alex] He was persecuting the Way, as the Bible says.

[Jordan] He was persecuting the way. That's right. And Jesus appears to him as the resurrected Lord. And immediately, this man who was a vehement enemy of Christians, the followers of Jesus, became one of our greatest champions. That missionary to the Gentiles dedicates his entire life to Jesus. What enemy does that?

[Alex] Right. And I think what's interesting in the case of Paul is even where people would say, and I've seen some atheists today say this, they'll say, well, clearly Paul is an intelligent person. I mean, he was part of the Pharisees. He was a brilliant scholar, just incredibly intelligent. And they'll say the only thing that could make him follow Jesus this way is if he had some sort of mental breakdown or a traumatic experience. They might say, maybe it did happen on the road to Damascus. He had a traumatic experience that caused him to go crazy, and he became a Jesus follower. What's interesting about that, though, is you see the same rationality he had beforehand as you do after he becomes a Jesus follower. He's just as rational. He's just as logical. And what's even more interesting is that it's like his eyes are finally open. And he'd go on to say this in 2 Corinthians chapters two and three, where he's like, for a while, it was like we had this veil over our eyes, but because of Jesus, the veil has been torn away, and we're seeing with clear eyes now. What's amazing, what I'm getting at here, is that he was a Jewish scholar. He was a Pharisee. And he would go on in Philippians chapter three to say, I was a Hebrew of Hebrews. I was your guy, blameless before the law. And when he understands that Jesus is the Messiah, and then he begins to look back on the Old Testament, he goes, it makes sense. It makes total sense. This is not someone who lost his mind or had a traumatic experience or a mental breakdown. This man met the risen Lord Jesus Christ, and everything made sense after that.

[Jordan] Yeah. And I think that's really the point we're getting at with this, too. It's what makes Easter such a celebratory time for us. Because, as we started just a bit ago in this podcast, the resurrection is everything for Christianity. Without it, nothing else matters. For Paul, he thought it was following the law at first until he met the resurrected Jesus. And then everything changed for him. I think that can be said for all of us, right?

[Alex] Yeah. And I mean, that's going to be my message this Sunday: that the resurrection changes everything for us.

[Jordan] And we don't need to be afraid to look into it. We should be excited. I'm a youth pastor. I always tell my students never to be afraid to ask questions.

[Alex] Yeah, because here's the thing. Those questions are going to be asked of you. And I know Christians who are afraid to listen to atheists give talks. I know Christians who are afraid to listen to anybody debate a Christian or question anything about the Bible, about the resurrection, because they're like, oh no, I guess what if they're right or what if they prove me wrong or something? And I always want to encourage Christians by saying we already know what the Bible says and the Bible is our ultimate authority. And so we don't have to worry about anything else. There's no atheist who's going to disprove the faith. Why? Because the faith is true.

[Jordan] I mean, there are even modern stories of that happening with some of our most famous modern scholars, right? CS Lewis tried to do that. Lee Strobel tried to debunk the very resurrection of Jesus. And what did it do when he dove into the evidence? It converted him.

[Alex] He became a believer.

[Jordan] He became a believer and wrote a book called The Case for Christ, which is about the pieces of evidence of the resurrection. We don't need to be afraid of it. We should dive into these things because they will always point us to the truth.

[Alex] Right. Yeah. Since God's word is ultimate truth, there's nothing that's going to contradict it and prove it to be false. I mean, obviously, things will go against it. People will raise objections to it. But at the end of the day, as we've just done here, we've just listed all of the main objections to the resurrection and all the ways it's tried to be dismissed today. And we've shown how they all fall flat. At the end of the day, what makes the most sense of literally all the evidence presented is that Jesus Christ rose from the dead by the power of God. And that ultimate truth is found in Scripture. And so I think we have a very firm foundation. I think we have great reasons to believe in the resurrection.

[Jordan] Definitely.

[Alex] Yeah. So, just trying to wrap this up, why should we believe in the resurrection?
First and foremost, the Bible says Jesus rose from the dead. Also, we know that Jesus died on the cross for our sins and that He was dead. Once He was definitely dead, they put Him in a tomb, and there was absolutely no way for Him to get Himself out of that tomb while He was dead. There was also no way for anyone else to get Him out of that tomb, nor would they have wanted to because it would have defeated their purposes entirely. And so what makes the most sense is that Jesus rose from the dead. And then we also have the validation of the post-resurrection appearances where He appeared to people like women, which you would not have made up if you were trying to make up a story. He appeared to fishermen, everyday normal people, and people who were trying to persecute His people and His mission and His church, and their lives were dramatically changed. And again, I'll get into this Sunday morning for my sermon, but ultimately, what ends

up changing people's hearts is not evidence. It's Jesus. It's a personal encounter with Jesus.

[Jordan] Yep. And it's just like if you were a judge in a court-room and you had the evidence laid before you, you then, as the judge, have to make that decision of what you do with this evidence. For the resurrection, the pieces of evidence are there. And every single one of us is going to be confronted with that evidence if we're willing to look into it and see, like you said, all logic, all evidence, all of it points to the most obvious answer being that Jesus did rise from the dead. He came out of that grave. So it falls on all of us. What do we do with that evidence? What do we decide to do with it?

[Alex] For those who don't believe, we hope this amount of evidence will encourage you to read the Bible to search Jesus out for yourself because I think this evidence can captivate your mind. I think it can challenge some notions that you hold to now. It can confront some beliefs that you have now. And when you experience that, that should force you and cause you to seek out Jesus in search of ultimate truth. And if you are a believer, what we hope it does is simply encourage your faith.

[Jordan] Yeah, that would encourage your faith and then make you want to tell others, right? That's what it did for all the followers of Jesus. If you truly do believe that Jesus rose from the dead, that's not something you keep to yourself.

[Alex] That's right. This is life-changing news.

[Jordan] Exactly. You're going to, you're going to have to tell somebody, you're going to have to do something about it.

[Alex] Yeah. So, we really do hope that this has been a helpful podcast for you. We wanted to do this around Easter. We wanted to, you know, just answer this question. Why should we believe in the resurrection of Jesus? And I hope that you have been encouraged. I hope you have found this answer helpful, and I am excited that Jordan got to be with us for this episode. So, thanks, Jordan, for coming on.

[Jordan] Yeah, it's been a blast. I love getting to talk about this stuff and just getting to hang out with you.

[Alex] Yeah. We'll probably do another one in the future.

[Jordan] It's gonna be awesome.

Chapter 14

Do Christians Need to Go to Priests?

✝

I think there are a couple of different ways to phrase this to try to get to the point of the question. You could say, do Christians need priests to intercede for them? Or do Christians need to go to priests for confession and forgiveness? Now, let me just say a word to the evangelical Christians in America. This question might not pique your interest because we really have no involvement with priests as evangelical Protestant Christians in America. However, this question is of great interest to many Christians around the world because, in other parts of the world, there are priests for hire. You see this a lot in Asian countries, for instance. Essentially, there are priests who say if you pay them a certain fee, they will pray to God on your behalf. They're doing this because they're portraying themselves as having some sort of special access to God that other people do not have. So, by paying them, they will go to God for you, and you can be certain that your prayers are heard. Unfortunately, many people end up paying them for this.

We also have to keep in mind the many Catholics in the world today who go to a priest literally every single week to confess their sins and receive the formal remission of sin imparted by the priest. It's called the sacrament of penance.[28] The priest will then tell the person what they must do to receive the forgiveness fully. They'll say something like, say ten Our Fathers and three Hail Marys, and then your sins will be absolutely forgiven. So, while most evangelical Protestants in America might not struggle with this issue, there are many Christians throughout the world who are seeing this practice take place, and there are many Catholics around the world who are engaging in it every single week.

Therefore, we once again must ask, what does the Bible say about it? Do Christians need priests to pray on their behalf? We need to get some clarification here for a second. We need to understand the difference between praying *for* somebody and praying *on behalf* of somebody. Praying for someone is lifting up another person in prayer to God. Praying on behalf of someone is serving as a mediator between that person and God. It's essentially like saying the other person doesn't have the access to God that you have. They don't have the right to approach God, and so you must do it in their place.

Praying for someone is entirely biblical. We see countless examples of this throughout the New Testament. If you think about the letters of Paul, Paul would often start his letters by telling the church that he remembers them in his prayers always. The Bible even says in James 5:16 that we are to pray for one another. In the letter to the Colossians, Paul specifically asked the church in Colossae to pray for him and those ministering with him. So praying for other Christians is not only biblical, it's a command. However, praying *on behalf* of someone, serving as a mediator for that person, is entirely unbiblical for Christians today. And there is a caveat there.

The reason that I say *today* is because in the Old Testament, a certain group of people did have the biblical, God-given responsibility of serving as mediators and praying on behalf of others. Those were the priests and the high priest. If you'll remember the priestly garments that Aaron, the first high priest, wore, you'll recall that he wore a breastplate, and on that breastplate were all 12 names of the tribes of Israel (Exodus 28:29). He would wear that breastplate as he made sacrifices and prayed to the Lord, and what he was doing was representing all 12 tribes to the Lord. He was serving as a mediator between those 12 tribes and God. He was going in between them. However, the reason this is unbiblical today is because Jesus fulfilled the role of the great high priest, and He continues to serve in that office today (Hebrews 7). The Bible says that He is a priest forever in the order of Melchizedek (Hebrews 7:17).

So, there is no biblical warrant for a person to serve as a mediator today. When Jesus died on the cross, you'll remember that the veil was torn. It was split in two. That veil was the curtain that separated the holy of holies from the rest of the temple. The holy of holies was the place where God met with man. It's where man and God met together, and no one could enter that place except for the high priest on the day of atonement. But now, because of Jesus, the Bible says in Hebrews 4:16 that we can approach the throne of God with boldness. You see, Jesus has eliminated the separation between God and man, so now we can approach God through Christ because the Bible says very plainly in 1 Timothy 2:5, "For there is one God and there is one mediator between God and men, the man, Jesus Christ."

Therefore, you do not need anyone other than Jesus Christ to mediate between you and God. You do not need a priest to pray on your behalf. If you are a Christian, you can go to the Father in prayer through Christ at any time because a priest does not have some special access to God that you do not have. The Bible teaches that every single believer is indwelt by the same Spirit of God. Every single believer is part of the royal priesthood (1 Peter 2:9). We have been made a kingdom of priests to our God through Christ. Therefore, every single believer has the exact same access to God as every other believer because our access is in and through Jesus Christ alone.

So, let's just say a few words about the Catholic practice of confession and the sacrament of penance. First and foremost, the ability to forgive sins belongs to God alone. Catholics will often go to a priest and confess their sins in order to be forgiven of their sins (or at least receive the formal remission of sins), but the ability to forgive sins belongs to God alone; even the Pharisees knew this. For as much as they got wrong and as often as they were opposing Jesus, even they knew this. When there was a man who was on a mat, and Jesus was telling him to get up and walk and take his mat and go home, Jesus said, "Son, your sins are forgiven." The Pharisees then said, "Who can forgive sins but God alone?" (Mark 2:5-7). You see, even they knew that only God can forgive sins. So, no priest has the ability to forgive your sins.

Second, the prescription given out by the priest is entirely unbiblical. Shouldn't it be concerning that priests today who claim to be the direct successors of the Apostles say and do things that the Apostles themselves never said or did? Should that not raise some red flags for us? When Peter finished his first sermon at Pentecost, the crowds asked him, "What must we do to be saved?" Peter did not prescribe any Our Fathers or Hail Marys. When Paul found out about the sinning that was going on in the church in Corinth and how they were tolerating it, he did not say, "Say five Our Fathers and two Hail Marys." He said to get rid of the sin that is within you. Put the one who refuses to stop sinning out of the fellowship until he repents and then receive him back with gladness. So, these prescriptions that are given out by priests today are entirely unbiblical and foreign to the Apostles themselves.

They're also unbiblical because the Lord's Prayer, the "Our Father," was given as a model prayer, not a prayer to be prayed as penance for sin. More importantly, you will never find anything in all of the Bible that says you are to pray to anyone but God alone. In fact, every time someone in Scripture prays to anyone else but the one true God, it is called blasphemy and idolatry. So do not pray to Mary. She cannot help you.

The third thing that we should say about Catholic practices has to do with confession. It's true that the Bible does command Christians to confess their sins to one another. We read about that in 1 John 1:9. We also read about it in James 5:16, but this is to occur between believers as a means of accountability and discipleship. You see, the Bible says that as the body of Christ, as believers, we're to do life with other believers who will be able to hold us accountable and help us live out the faith in a biblical manner. However, the Catholic practice eliminates these elements entirely because just think about how it's set up. You enter a confessional anonymously, and then there's a barrier between you and the priest so that he cannot see who is confessing. Well, that completely eliminates the accountability, the fellowship, and the discipleship that's supposed to take place within these relationships between Christians. So they're practicing a biblical command in an entirely unbiblical way.

So, let's just summarize some of these points. No Christian has more access to God than any other Christian. We all have the same access to God because it comes through Christ alone. So you don't need to go to someone to pray on your behalf. If you are a Christian, you have Christ, and you have the spirit of God dwelling in you, so you have the exact same access to God that any other Christian would have. So you don't need someone to pray on your behalf as a mediator because there is only one mediator between God and men, and that is Jesus Christ. You can go to God through Christ at any time, and you can actually do so boldly because of Christ's sacrifice on your behalf. Also, remember that the office of a priest has absolutely no basis in the New Testament whatsoever. Every single Christian is part of the royal priesthood. We have been made a kingdom of priests to our God.

Also, remember that God alone can forgive sins and pronounce the forgiveness of sins. No man can do that. The prescriptions given by priests today are entirely unbiblical. The call of the Bible is repentance, turning from your sins and committing yourself to Christ, not praying rote prayers as an act of penance. Finally, remember that confession is to occur within Christian relationships for accountability, fellowship, and discipleship. You don't need a priest; you only need Jesus, and praise God that we have Him. So, I hope you found this answer helpful, and as always, just dig into the Scriptures so that we can see what the Bible has to say about all these questions.

Chapter 15

What's the Significance of Jesus Entering Jerusalem from the East?

✝

This question is actually a question that was raised from a sermon that I preached. I was preaching a Palm Sunday sermon on Jesus' triumphal entry into Jerusalem, and in Matthew 21, the Bible says that Jesus entered Jerusalem from the East. I mentioned in the sermon how that phrase had a whole lot of biblical theology and so much good stuff to unpack, but unfortunately, I didn't have time in the sermon to mention everything that I wanted to. So I said, hey, if you're curious, submit the question to the podcast; I'd be happy to answer it. Thankfully, someone did. So we get to dive in and figure out what the significance of His entering Jerusalem from the East actually is. And we really need to understand that this has a lot to do with biblical theology.

For the answer, you actually have to go all the way back to the beginning of the Bible, all the way back to the book of Genesis, where we read in the beginning that God created mankind. He gives them this beautiful place called Eden. In the midst of Eden, there's a garden, and this garden served as a kind of first temple. It's a place where God and man could meet together, where mankind can enter into the Lord's presence. But as we continue reading, we know what happens. Adam and Eve rebelled and sinned against God. So the Lord banishes them from the garden. In reality, they are banished from the presence of the Lord. They no longer have the privilege of fellowship with the Lord. As we continue reading in Genesis chapter 3, the Bible says, "God places the cherubim with a flaming sword in the East of the garden." This means that if someone were to enter the garden, they must enter by the East. This becomes a theme throughout the book of Genesis.

You can actually track this phrase (to the east) and see the progression of people moving further away from the presence of God, further away from God's loving relationship, and towards sin. Even in the very next chapter of Genesis, in Genesis chapter 4, we read about how Cain kills his brother Abel. The Bible specifically says in Genesis 4:16, "Then Cain went away from the presence of the Lord and settled in the land of Nod, East of Eden." So again, we see the continuation of that idea that moving eastward is moving towards sin, towards rebellion, away from the presence of the Lord.

A few chapters after that, we read about Abraham and Lot. Their families and herds were growing so much that they could no longer dwell in the same land. So Abraham told Lot to pick whatever land he wanted, and Abraham would choose whatever land Lot didn't choose. So Lot lifts up his eyes and looks *to the east*, and he sees the land that he wants to settle in. It's actually the land of Sodom. So Lot moves further *towards the east*, further towards sin, further away from the presence of the Lord, and he ends up dwelling in a land of sin. We all know what happened to Sodom and Gomorrah. This theme continues not only throughout the book of Genesis but also throughout the Old Testament. Again, it's this idea that moving eastward is moving away from the presence of the Lord and towards sin and rebellion.

Then, we come to the New Testament. It's really interesting to see how the Old Testament and the New Testament both start. The Old Testament starts with mankind sinning against God and walking away from the presence of the Lord *to the East*. Interestingly, the New Testament starts with men coming *from the East* to the very presence of the Lord. Remember, Matthew 2:1 says, "Now after Jesus was born in Bethlehem of Judea in the days of Herod the king, behold, wise men from the east came to Jerusalem." Of course, we know that they announced to Herod that they had come to worship Him, who was born the King of the Jews. Don't miss that: you have people coming *from the east* to the very presence of God, to Jesus. It's the first sign that with the arrival of Jesus, sin's curse is being undone, that though mankind had sinned against God and were forced away from His presence, Jesus was bringing mankind back to God.

This is seen again in Jesus's triumphal entry. In Matthew 21, we read about Jesus's "triumphal entry," and it's interesting how the Gospel of Matthew has these bookends, right? The Gospel of Matthew begins with *wise men* coming *from the East* to worship *the king of the Jews,* and the whole city is *stirred*. Then, it begins its conclusion with a *wise man,* Jesus, coming *from the East* as *the king of the Jews*. The Bible even says in Matthew 21:10 that "the whole city was *stirred*." Therefore, Jesus entering Jerusalem from the East is the climactic resolution to the problem of sin that was started way back in the garden. His arrival was a sign of peace, that He was going to make peace between God and man, the peace that we need that was originally undone by mankind in the garden. Jesus was going to make this peace by paying for the very sins that caused enmity between God and man in the first place. It is a sign that Jesus is the true king with the authority and power to do what we cannot do for ourselves.

So, as I said, there's a whole lot of biblical theology here. The first Adam was our federal head, meaning he represented all of mankind. The first Adam disobeyed God and took us away from the presence of the Lord. The Bible refers to Jesus as the second Adam (Romans 5:12-21). The second Adam also served as our federal head, meaning Jesus represented us to God. We know the Bible says that He obeyed God perfectly and brought us back into the presence of the Lord by making peace by the blood of his cross (Colossians 1:20).

So you see, this is just one of those amazing times in Scripture where it's a very small detail that could easily be looked over but is crucially important for understanding redemptive history. This is what I love about the Bible. I love everything about it, but I love how God just packs all these amazing, wonderful details in His Word that are worthy of dwelling upon and thinking about if we would just take the time to do so. Because here's what I know. When most of us are going to read the story of the triumphal entry, we focus on all other sorts of details. That's understandable. It's good to focus on those as well. But we'll read a phrase like "Jesus entered Jerusalem from the east," and we just read right over it. We don't pay it any more attention or give it any other thought. But when we take the time to ask questions like, why was that included? Why did God find it necessary to include that little phrase? It wasn't an accident. It wasn't just something He threw in. Every word is intentional. When you begin to look at the theology of the East, and you track that phrase throughout the Bible, you begin to unpack all of these rich details about how it started all the way back in the garden.

Jesus entering Jerusalem from the east signifies that Jesus is returning us to God. The first Adam took us away from God, but the second Adam is bringing us back to God. The first Adam disrupted peace with God. The second Adam is establishing peace with God forever. The first Adam sinned against God, and his guilt was passed down to all of us, as well as his sin nature, meaning that all of us are going to incur the wrath of God. We deserve the wrath of God for our sins. But then we see that the second Adam comes, and He is going to pay the penalty for our sins so that He would take the wrath of God in our place and we could have peace with God through Him. All this comes from just taking time to dwell on that one phrase. I think our prayer should be that of the psalmist who said, "Open up our eyes to behold wondrous things from your word" (Psalm 119:18). So that's the significance of Jesus entering Jerusalem from the east.

Chapter 16

Do Christians Need at Least Two People for Jesus to be Present?

✝

"Where two or more are gathered, Jesus is there." That's a phrase that gets thrown around a lot today. It's actually pretty common to hear. The most common places that you'll hear this are in the context of a small gathering. It could be a small church gathering, it could be a prayer meeting, or it could be a Bible study. What typically happens is a person will notice how small the gathering is, and they'll try to encourage others by saying something like, well, we may be small in number, but that's okay because we know Jesus says, where two or three are gathered in my name, there I am among them.

That sounds like a nice encouragement, right? I would be encouraged. I've been a part of lots of small church gatherings, and hearing that is really encouraging. What's not so encouraging is when you begin to follow that statement to its logical conclusion, like, what if it's only me? What if I don't have another person? Is Jesus not present with me unless at least one other person is around? Does that mean that I can't have a personal relationship with Jesus? We begin to see a big problem here. It's one that you're going to encounter a lot today. It's the type of problem that occurs when we rip verses out of their context.

You see, one of the worst and most dangerous things anyone can do is take verses from the Bible out of their context because context is king. The context of a verse determines the meaning of a verse. So, we need to dig into the context of this verse in order to know how to understand it properly. This phrase, where two or three are gathered, actually comes from Matthew chapter 18:15-20. This is what the Bible says, starting in verse 15.

> If your brother sins against you, go and tell him his fault between you and him alone. If he listens to you, you've gained your brother. But if he does not listen, take one or two others along with you, that every charge may be established by the evidence of two or three witnesses. If he refuses to listen to them, tell it to the church. If he refuses to listen even to the church, let him be to you as a Gentile and a tax collector. Truly, I say to you, whatever you bind on earth shall be bound in heaven, and whatever you loose on earth shall be loosed in heaven. Again, I say to you, if two of you agree on earth about anything they ask, it will be done for them by my Father in heaven. For where two or three are gathered in my name, there am I among them.

This passage is actually about church discipline. Jesus is instructing His followers about what to do when there is sin in the church. To combat the problem of sin in the church, He gives a number of steps for the church discipline process that are incredibly helpful. He says, step one, if someone is in the church and they're sinning, and you know that they're sinning and they're living in this habitual, unrepentant sin, you go to the person yourself. You go one-on-one, and you talk with them. But, step two, if that person doesn't listen to you, take one or two others so that whatever your judgment may be, it will be established by the witness of two or three people. So notice the use of that exact same phrase, *two or three*.

The reason for needing two or three witnesses was to be in accordance with the law of God. The Bible says in Deuteronomy 19:15, "A single witness shall not suffice against a person for any crime or for any wrong in connection with the offense that he has committed. Only on the evidence of two witnesses or of three witnesses shall a charge be established." You see, what Jesus is doing here is continuing this practice within the church with regard to church discipline. He says in order for a charge to be valid and established, there must be at least two or three witnesses. One witness alone is insufficient to establish the charge against a person.

So then, step three, He says if the person still refuses to listen, you must then present him to the church. Finally, step number four, if he refuses even to listen to the church, he is to be put out of the church and treated as an unbeliever until the time in which he repents. You actually see this kind of discipline process in 1 Corinthians chapter 5. In that chapter, Paul is addressing a serious sin that is ongoing in the church. The church did not put the person out of the church as they were supposed to. So Paul says, stop tolerating the sin of this person. Put them out of the church. Give them time to repent, and receive them back gladly if that person does repent. Interestingly, there's actually evidence from 2 Corinthians that the person Paul addressed in 1 Corinthians did repent, so we see that person gain membership back into the church and is welcomed back into the church after he repents. This process of discipline and restoration is exactly what Jesus is talking about in Matthew 18. Jesus concludes these verses with the phrase, "Where two or three are gathered, there am I among them," to *legitimize* and *confirm* the church discipline process.

You see, unfortunately, we're living in a time in which very few churches today even practice church discipline, even though it is a biblical command and even though it is necessary, which is one of the main reasons the church today is in the state that it's in. Because we are not practicing church discipline, we're allowing people to live in habitual, unrepentant sin. We're not calling them out on their sin. We're not going and talking with them. We're not following the church discipline process. So, our churches become filled with sin. Also, you end up having a lot of unbelievers become members in the church who shouldn't be members in the church because they haven't actually repented of their sins and come to faith in Christ. We need church discipline in order to have a pure church. That doesn't mean that people are going to be perfect, but it does mean that we actually care that they are growing in holiness, that we care about their sanctification and their growth in Christ.

Also, here's what I know: one of the most common responses when you are a church practicing church discipline is that people will protest. If you're actually going to practice church discipline and you're going to go through this process, there's going to be backlash. Accusations are going to be thrown around. The one who is being disciplined often accuses the pastoral leadership of tyranny, of being authoritarian, maybe even acting as hypocrites. In this passage, Jesus is anticipating this kind of response, so He says, actually, I stand by their judgment. If they have followed the process and their judgment is established on the basis of at least two or three witnesses, I stand alongside them and their judgment. I agree with them. If they have followed this process on earth, it is bound up in heaven. It has the heavenly authority behind it.

So Jesus is saying, I stand with them in this process. It is not an act of tyranny. It is not an act of authoritarian leadership or even hypocrites or anything like that. Jesus is saying, I stand with them. This is a legitimate process, and I am giving my authority and approval to it.

We need to stop ripping this verse and other verses out of their context because when we do that, we misapply it today. This is not an encouragement for small gatherings. I'm not saying small gatherings are bad at all. I love small gatherings. They're some of the sweetest times you can have, but this verse says nothing about small gatherings. It is not an encouragement for small gatherings. It shouldn't be used to apply to small gatherings. On the plus side, it does mean that you don't have to worry about always needing at least one other person in order for Jesus to be present. You can be sure that if you're a believer in Jesus, Jesus is always with you, and that is an encouragement.

Chapter 17

What is the Meaning of 666?

✝

That's a good question, and it's one I'm sure that's going to be of interest to people because it comes from the Book of Revelation. Pretty much anything from the book of Revelation is of interest to people today. The number 666 comes from Revelation 13:11-18, which is a section about the beast and his false prophet. Specifically, the number occurs in verse 18. This is what the Bible says in Revelation 13:18, "This calls for wisdom. Let the one who has understanding calculate the number of the beast, for it is the number of a man, and his number is 666." Basically, we read that, and we're supposed to understand that in some way, the number 666 is a clue to the identity of the beast, which, of course, means that naturally, a lot of people throughout history have tried to attribute some sort of numerical value to letters in order to figure out the identity or a name for the referent of this number.

Throughout history, numerous suggestions have been made about who people think the beast is based on that person's name (or title) and the numerical value it produces. For instance, one of the most common suggestions throughout history has been the pope. Many people will suggest the pope is the referent to this number for many reasons. One reason, in particular, is that the pope is referred to as Vicarious Filii Dei, the vice-regent of the son of God. Interestingly enough, when you add up the numerical value of that title, it equals 666. People have done this with names like Ronald Wilson Reagan, Mikhail Gorbachev, Hitler, Vespasian, and Domitian. People have always found a way to make certain names equal the numerical value 666.[29.] Arguably, though, the most popular suggestion is the name Nero.

Many people today are absolutely insistent that 666 has to refer to Nero, the first-century Roman emperor. There is a case to be made for Nero, considering the fact that he was an emperor in the first century, and he fits well with the historical context of the book of Revelation. Furthermore, many people have pointed out that adding up the numerical value of Nero's title equals 666. So, there is something to be said for Nero as a suggestion. However, the big problem with suggesting Nero is that his name only equals 666 under very specific conditions.

First, you have to use the specific name and title "Nero Caesar," even though there were many other versions and titles of Nero's name.[30] Second, you have to use the Greek version of Nero Caesar, which is "Neron Caesar," because the Latin version, which was much more commonly used in that day, only adds up to 616.[31] Not only do you have to use the Greek version of his name, Neron Caesar, you then have to use Hebrew letters to represent the name. Keep in mind that the Hebrew alphabet assigns a numerical value to their letters. So when Neron Caesar is spelled using Hebrew letters, the value of those letters equals 666 exactly.[32]

But here's the question, folks: Did John, under the inspiration of the Holy Spirit, really intend for us to understand Nero as the referent? Intend for us to know to use the specific title,

Nero Caesar? Intend for us to specifically know to use the Greek version of his name, Neron Caesar, rather than the more commonly used Latin version of his name? And then intend for us to know to represent that name in Hebrew letters so that it would equal 666? Maybe.

However, that does seem unlikely, doesn't it? I think the big problem with this whole issue regarding the number is the approach. Revelation 13:18 says there is a call for wisdom. We need wisdom to discern the meaning of the number and its referent. However, so far, we have committed ourselves to intellectual wisdom, seeking to assign numerical value to various letters in order to try to discern the identity of its referent. As we have seen, doing that leads to innumerable possibilities. Given the right configuration, You can make almost any name equal to the number 666.

So maybe the wisdom we need isn't necessarily *intellectual* wisdom here. Maybe the wisdom that John is saying we need is *spiritual* wisdom. That would actually fit well within the context of the entire book of Revelation. Throughout the book of Revelation, the ones who conquer, the ones who win the victory, and the ones who make it to the end are not the intellectually superior but the faithful.[33] It seems then that faithfulness, not intelligence, is the key to seeing through the deception of the Antichrist. Keep in mind that is what the Antichrist is trying to do. He is trying to deceive people, so John says we need wisdom. Naturally, our minds assume that wisdom refers to intellectual wisdom. When in reality, it seems more likely that what we actually need is spiritual wisdom that would push us towards faithfulness to Christ.

So maybe we need a new way of looking at the number entirely. If we aren't going to come to a specific name when looking at the number, what will we make of it when we read it? When you're reading Revelation 13, you come to the number, what are we supposed to make of it? There's no denying that

Revelation is arguably the most symbolic book in the Bible, and it uses numbers symbolically throughout the book. For instance, the number seven is often used as the number of perfection. It's said to be God's number because He is perfect. That would mean the number six is just shy of perfection, right? Many have suggested that the number six is the number of mankind.[34] God created man on which day? The sixth day. Interestingly enough, if you read Revelation 13:18 in Greek, it says that this number is the number of man. Some of your translations will say it is the number of "a" man, but in Greek, it just says it's the number of man. So, six is a number that represents falling short. It's a number that represents being incomplete. The fact that it's repeated three times, 666, is to portray total and complete insufficiency and incompleteness.

In contrast, in Revelation, the heavenly host declare God to be "holy, holy, holy" (Revelation 4:8). He's not just called holy once; no, He's called holy three times. Why? Because he is perfectly and completely holy. So, the beast is called 666 because he falls short of who he pretends to be. He sets out to deceive humanity into thinking that he is Christ. He will seek to deceive with his teaching and with his so-called miracles, but the point that the Bible is making here is that he falls short of the one true Christ. Therefore, we're not supposed to know the identity, and we're not supposed to focus on trying to figure out the identity. That's not because God's trying to hide things from us. It's because He doesn't want us to get distracted from the very thing we need to be able to recognize the beast when he comes, which is a total devotion to Christ.

You see if we spend all our time obsessing over the identity of 666 and we try all sorts of names, it actually takes away from our devotion and commitment to Jesus. It takes away from our time with Jesus. The best way to identify a counterfeit check is to be completely familiar with authentic checks, right? If you want to know what a counterfeit looks like, you have to know what the authentic thing looks like. In the same way, the best way to identify a false Christ is to know the authentic Christ intimately.

So yes, we do need wisdom, but we need spiritual wisdom, which does not obsess over identifying the referent of 666 but focuses on growing closer to Jesus so that we will be able to recognize the false Christ when he comes. That's what 666 is all about. It refers to a beast who is coming, an antichrist who will seek to deceive the world into thinking that he is the true Christ. The only way to see through that deception is not with a superior intellect but with a complete devotion to Christ. So, once again, focus on Jesus. Focus on your relationship with Him, growing closer to Him. Know the authentic Christ so well that no false Christ could possibly deceive you.

Chapter 18

Has Science Disproven God?

†

That's an interesting question. Let me just say at the beginning, I really do appreciate the fact that it was posed as a question because typically, when I have encountered this issue, it has been asserted as a claim. I've been in contexts before I was a pastor when I was working in secular jobs, and I would be talking with someone, and they'd find out I was a believer, and they'd say, how can you be a believer? How can you believe in God? Don't you know that science has disproven God? It's meant to be a derogatory, condescending comment, basically saying that Christians are unintelligent and that we're foolish for believing in God in an age in which most people believe that science has eliminated the need for God. Christians, you are going to encounter this topic at some point in your walk. You're going to engage with someone. It could be at work or in some other kind of context. You're going to engage with someone who's going to bring up this topic. So we need to know how to handle this topic when it comes our way.

Let me start by giving you a little tactic that I like to use. If you ever encounter someone who says to you, science has disproven God, my favorite response and my church even knows what I'm about to say, my favorite response is to say, "What do you mean by that?" I learned about this tactic by reading Greg Koukl's amazing book called *Tactics*.[35] One reason it's my favorite response is that most people in our world today make assertions with no backing, and we, for whatever reason, have learned to just accept whatever assertions a person makes without questioning them. For instance, someone will say to us science has disproven God, and we typically just accept that as a fact. We move on, or we might say, that's your opinion, but I still believe the Bible. We're just accepting something they have offered no proof or backing for. That statement science has disproven God is an unproven assertion. So one reason I like to respond with, "What do you mean by that?" is because now that person actually has to defend their position.

The other reason that this is such a fun response is because most people who make assertions haven't actually thought through the assertions they make. They just know that "science has disproven God" is a talking point. It's something that many atheists say today; it's something that most of the world accepts today, but they haven't even given it the thought necessary to defend that kind of assertion. Most people have not thought through their own positions or beliefs, so they don't know how to defend them. That's another reason why this question is so fun just to pose the question, well, what do you mean by that?

So, I want to encourage you, first and foremost, to learn to recognize undefended assertions and then, secondly, make people defend their own assertions. If someone's going to make a claim and they don't offer any backing for it whatsoever, they just state it as a bold assertion, make them defend their position, and see what they can do. As I said, if you're a believer, you're going to encounter this topic at some point, and the question is, what do you mean by that? Can only get you so far. So, we need to learn how to engage in this conversation.

It's helpful when you have someone making that claim, "science has disproven God," to figure out in what ways they imagine science has disproven God. In other words, in what particular ways has science disproven God? What in our modern scientific understanding has eliminated the possibility or the necessity of God's existence? Because science is a broad umbrella, right? It's a very broad range of fields, so it's really helpful to try to figure out in what ways a person might think that science has eliminated the need for God.

For most people who make this kind of a claim, it's going to come down to one issue and one issue only, the dreaded E word: evolution. Many will say that evolution disproves God, and we're going to address that more thoroughly in just a little while, but for now, we need to understand that the theory of evolution is just that it's a theory. More than that, evolution can only explain how life has arrived at the point it is now. In other words, evolution can say nothing and does say nothing about how life began. For you to have a theory of evolution and even have that conversation, you already have to have life existing. At that point (when life already exists), evolution seeks to explain how something got from point A to point B over a long period of time and through a series of random processes. That leaves people with a huge problem. We can have the evolution discussion, but before that, we have to determine where life begins in the first place.

There's no scientific consensus today about *how* everything came into being or even *why* everything came into being. You have to answer and deal with that question before you can even begin discussing evolution. In order to deal with this problem, scientists for many years have posited that the universe must be eternal. If you want to explain *why* there is something rather than nothing and *how* there is something rather than nothing, the easiest way around that is to say that the universe has always existed. It is eternal, so nothing brought it into existence or, specifically in our case, no one brought it into existence because they say it's always existed. However, science itself has proven this false in many different ways. For instance, the second law of thermodynamics states that in a closed system, the amount of usable energy decreases over time.[36] If the universe were eternal, all of the usable energy in the universe would have already been expended, resulting in a state of maximum entropy where nothing could happen. Since things are still happening in the universe, this implies to us that the universe has not always existed.

Another key way we know that the universe is not eternal is the expansion of the universe. Observations of distant galaxies show us that they are moving away from us at a rate proportional to their distance.[37] This suggests to us that the universe is expanding. If the universe had existed forever, it would have expanded infinitely, making it infinite in size. However, observations show that the universe has a finite size, suggesting that it has not always existed. Another way to think about this is that things expand outward from the point of origin, which means that since the universe is expanding, it must have a starting point. If you throw a rock into a lake or some other body of water, you can see the ripples expanding outward from the point where the rock hits the surface of the water. So, the fact that the universe is expanding outward means that it had a starting point from which it began to expand.

Another key observation that lets us know the universe is not eternal is the cosmic microwave background radiation. The cosmic microwave background radiation is the Big Bang's afterglow and is the universe's oldest light. It provides strong evidence that the universe had a beginning.[38] If the universe were eternal, no cosmic microwave background radiation would exist. This comes back to the idea of the Big Bang. When the idea of the Big Bang was first posited in 1931, many people thought it was going to be the death knell for religious believers. However, it's done just the opposite.

If the universe is eternal and has always existed, it would be a death knell to religion. It would even contradict the Bible because the very first verse in the Bible is, "In the beginning, God created the heavens and the earth" (Genesis 1:1). Well, that's false if the universe has always existed. If the universe is eternal, it would undermine our faith entirely, but if the universe did begin to exist, as we know it did, that would cause a lot more problems for scientists than it does for Christians. Because now, scientists have to explain *why* there is something rather than nothing and *how* there is something rather than nothing. And let me just tell you, no scientific theories today adequately answered those two questions of *why* there is something rather than nothing and *how* there is something rather than nothing.

That's not to say that scientists have not tried to explain it. Many have. For instance, the great biologist, Darwinian evolutionist, and fervent atheist Richard Dawkins proposed that aliens are the solution for life on Earth. He actually said this in an interview. When he was asked how life began on Earth, he said it was possible that another life form more intelligent and further along than us seeded life on this planet.[39] When asked about that alien species, he said that they too must have evolved by some Darwinian means. However, that doesn't answer the question of where that life form came from to begin with. You could say that they were seeded by even another life form, but eventually, you have to account for the origin of the first life form, the first intelligent life. Therefore, his solution fails. He might explain our existence by aliens and those aliens' existence by other aliens, but eventually, you have to explain how the first life forms were created. How did they come into being? What is their origin?

Another suggestion is proposed by the renowned chemist and atheist Peter Atkins, who is also a very fervent atheist (all the people I'm going to mention are atheists). He's written about his theory for *why* and *how* we have something rather than nothing. He says that nothing rolled over into some-thing.[40.] If you want clarification, you won't find much from him. He tried to explain this theory. He's written about it. He talked about it in an interview. He said that there was noth-ing, and then, at some point, "nothing rolled over into some-thing."[41] That is his scientific explanation for *why* and *how* there is something rather than nothing. The idea is so fantas-tical and unscientific that it, too, can be easily dismissed.

However, there's the suggestion from Lawrence Krauss, a famous physicist, and atheist. He proposed a much more likely theory, a very strong contender. Lawrence Krauss wrote a book called A *Universe From Nothing* because he knew that the data says that there was nothing, and then there was something. So he seeks to answer that question: How can something come from nothing? His solution was dark matter. He proposed that the existence of dark matter could theoretically bring about the existence of our universe.[42] However, I hope you can rec-ognize the difference between a universe *from nothing* and a universe *from the nonvisible* because that's what dark matter is. It's nonvisible. We can't see it, but that doesn't make it nothing. It makes it unseen. If we really want an answer to *how* something comes from nothing, we have to truly start with nothing, including the existence of dark matter. That's what nothing is. It means there is nothing there.

Another suggestion is the theory of the late Stephen Hawk-ing, arguably the most famous and important scientist of the last 100 years. His solution to the problem of the origins of the universe was gravity. He wrote, "Because there is such a law like gravity the universe can and will create itself from nothing...Spontaneous creation is the reason there is something rather than nothing, why the universe exists, why we exist."[43] But again, I want you to notice how that commits the same error as Krauss's theory. If there was truly nothing at some point, then not even gravity existed, and if gravity didn't exist, then there was no law of gravity. Something, in this case, gravity, cannot be the *cause* of bringing into existence the very thing needed to cause *its own* existence. You can't say because we have a law of gravity, a universe can and will create itself when we're talking about a place in time when there was nothing. If there was nothing, there was no gravity, there was no law of gravity, and therefore, the universe cannot create itself in that way.

These are the major theories in science today as to how the universe began to exist, and they all fail miserably. Science has not and cannot explain *how* and *why* there is something rather than nothing. Looking at the problem scientifically, you begin to realize that the solution of the Christians, being that there is a God in heaven who brought the universe into existence, seems to be a *better fit* and *more plausible* than any of the major scientific theories that we have today. The Christian solution makes better sense of the available data.

When someone's trying to have this conversation about science disproving God, I encourage you to go back to the very beginning. Go back to the problem of origins and try to have them explain *why* and *how* there is something rather than nothing. They won't be able to do it, and what they're going to do is try to transition into a conversation about evolution. So, let's begin to think about life in the universe after it began to exist. We're confronted now with the problem of evolution, and many people today think that the theory of evolution definitely disproves God, so we need to address it.

As I said earlier, it's important to remember that evolution is just a theory, which means it hasn't been proven. As much as people act like it has been, as much as teachers and education systems want to act as though it has been proven, it is still just a theory. Interestingly, though, many mainstream scientists are becoming increasingly disillusioned with the current Darwinian model of evolution because there are a number of problems with the theory of evolution as it's presented today that people just tend to look over or people aren't familiar with. They just know what they are told and regurgitate that back to us. So, the first problem with Darwinian evolution is the astronomical improbability of life being able to form according to the Darwinian model of evolution. In order to have life, you need the basic building blocks of life, which are things like proteins, amino acids, and enzymes. Without these things, you cannot have life.

Well, if you listen to most evolutionists talk, they believe that our world, in the beginning, consisted primarily of a primordial soup. The whole world was just a wasteland of this primordial soup. From that soup, life emerged. The problem, however, is that liquid is a terrible environment to form enzymes. The National Academy of Sciences acknowledges that "two amino acids do not spontaneously join in water. Rather, the opposite reaction is thermodynamically favored."[44] Essentially, water breaks protein chains down into amino acids or other constituents, making it difficult to produce proteins or other polymers in the primordial soup. Therefore, it is highly unlikely that these things began to form, given the environment in which evolutionists say our world consisted of in the beginning of this primordial soup.

Furthermore, it's still nearly impossible even in the most ideal conditions. In fact, there was an evolutionary scientist who formulated a model to calculate the probability for the formation, not just of one enzyme molecule but the smallest likely living organism by random processes. He found the probability, given the most ideal environment, he found the probability to be one chance in 10 to the 340 millionth power; in case you're wondering, that's 10 with 340 million zeros behind it.[45]

Here's an analogy to help us understand this kind of probability. This would be like placing a one-inch target on Pluto and then standing on Earth and shooting a rifle into space and hitting that one-inch target on Pluto. It is so improbable that it is essentially impossible. And yet, this is the very model that is being touted as undeniable certainty. This is the very model that's being taught in schools and the very model that we're not supposed to question and that we get made fun of for questioning.

Another big problem with the theory of evolution is the lack of transitional fossils. The theory of evolution claims that members of one species slowly evolve over time to become a new species. I mean, the famous example of this is of chimps slowly evolving into humans. Given that this theory states that everything in the world today has evolved in this way over time, you would think that there would be an abundance of transitional fossils. Basically, the fossils of the various species in between what they were to what they eventually become. However, we don't have those transitional fossils. In fact, one zoology textbook observed that "many species remain virtually unchanged for millions of years, then suddenly disappear to be replaced by quite different, but related form. Moreover, most major groups of animals appear abruptly in the fossil record, fully formed and with no fossils yet discovered that form a transition from their parent group."[46] I mean, even that zoology textbook is admitting that when you look at the fossil record, you find these species that appear abruptly, and there are no transitional species that lead to the species that we find.

However, if Darwinian evolution is true, you would expect there to be an abundance of transitional fossils. This perplexed Darwin himself. He thought that when we searched the oldest layers of the fossil record, we would find single-celled organisms and would be able to track their evolution throughout the fossil layers. However, what we actually discovered in the oldest layers of the fossil record was an explosion of fully formed multi-celled organisms with no biological ancestors.[47] This undermines Darwin's theory completely. He proposed that we would find this single-celled organism, and we'd be able to track it throughout its evolutionary process to become what it eventually would become. And yet, when we look at the oldest layers of the fossil record today, we have an abundance of multi-cell organisms with no ancestors in the fossil layers.

However, maybe the biggest problem with Darwinian evolution is that of what is called irreducible complexity. Now, I don't know if you've ever heard of that before, so let me explain. Irreducible complexity is the concept that some biological systems are so complex that they cannot be explained by gradual step-by-step evolution.[48]

Another way to think about it is that certain biological systems require all of their components in order to function, so they could not evolve step-by-step as the theory of evolution claims. One of the most famous examples of this is the bacterial flagellum, a microcellular rotary engine functioning like an outboard motor on bacteria to propel it through a liquid medium to find food. The flagellum is irreducibly complex. It fails to assemble or function properly if any one of its approximately 35 genes is missing. Mutations cannot produce the complexity needed to provide a functional flagellar rotary engine one incremental step at a time.[49] Essentially, this flagellum cannot function without all of its components being present at one time and functioning at one time.

However, evolution, especially the Darwinian model of evolution, says that it would gradually get these components over time, but it would not be able to function or continue to evolve without having them all. This is the problem of irreducible complexity. It's such a big problem that Darwin himself was actually worried about this possibility. You see this in his famous work, *On The Origin of the Species*. He said, "If it could be demonstrated that any complex organ existed, which could not possibly have been formed by numerous successive slight modifications, my theory would absolutely break down."[50]

I don't know why we're ignoring that today. I don't know why people are acting like we're crazy when we deny Darwinian evolution. I don't know why people today are acting like we're the foolish ones when we say that we doubt Darwinian evolution because Darwin himself said that if you could find this thing (irreducible complexity, specifically an organism that is irreducibly complex), his theory would absolutely break down, and we have found it. There are a number of examples, but the bacterial flagellum is demonstrably irreducibly complex and cannot evolve in the Darwinian model. So, his theory does break down. Darwin himself admitted that and yet most people today ignore his concerns entirely. The fact that we have discovered multiple irreducibly complex organisms completely undermines the theory of evolution.

We could say much more about this issue, and we probably will in an upcoming episode, but suffice it to say that science has not disproven God. I know that's a common claim made today, but remember, we must challenge claims. We need to challenge undefended assertions, make people defend their positions, and make others explain why and how there is something rather than nothing.

Chapter 19

What is the Best Bible Translation?

✝

Unfortunately, this is incredibly difficult to answer. You see, when it comes to Bible translation, the basic common goal of all translations is to help us understand in our language what was originally written in a different language.

There are three basic approaches in order to accomplish that goal. One approach is referred to as formal equivalence, which is also known as the word-for-word approach. As its name implies, this approach seeks to accurately express in one language what was written in a different language.[51] This approach tends to give preference to *accuracy* over *clarity*. For instance, let's take a passage such as Amos 4:6. In Hebrew, it uses an obscure phrase. In the Hebrew, it literally says, "cleanness of teeth." Word-for-word translations translate that exact phrase into English using the appropriate English words. So, you end up with a word-for-word equivalent. These translations say, "cleanness of teeth." With these translations, you might not know what the Bible *means*, but you will know what the Bible *says*. Common word-for-word translations that are used today are translations such as the NASB, which is the New American Standard Bible, the ESV, which is the English Standard Version, the KJV, and the NKJV. The major benefit of this approach is that you get to see in English what is communicated or written in the original Aramaic, Hebrew, or Greek text. The greatest benefit to this approach is that it is accurate to the original languages. The con to this approach is that sometimes you don't actually know what is meant by the words used in the original language. For instance, with our example from Amos chapter four, the phrase "cleanness of teeth," you will know that what you're reading is exactly what the originals say, but you won't necessarily know what that phrase is seeking to communicate.

Another approach that's taken today in Bible translation is the dynamic equivalent approach, otherwise known as the thought-for-thought approach. This approach gives preference to *clarity* over *accuracy*. In this approach, the goal is not always to accurately represent the words of one language with the words of another language but rather to accurately communicate the *thought* or the *idea* behind what was written.[52] With this approach, even though the Hebrew of Amos 4:6 might say "cleanness of teeth," it would not be translated that way with these particular versions. Instead, they would translate the phrase as "famine" because that's the idea being expressed by the phrase "cleanness of teeth." They understand that such a phrase is unfamiliar to us today. Therefore, they seek to help us out by telling us what the phrase means. With this approach, you might not always know what the Bible *says* exactly, but you will know what it *means*. Some of the common thought-for-thought translations used today are the CSB, which is the Christian Standard Bible, the NIV, the New International Version, the NAB, which is the New American Bible, and the NET, which is the New English Translation. The pros of this approach are that it makes the Bible easy to read, and you'll typically know the thought behind obscure words and phrases, which is great. However, the major con of this approach is that you won't actually know what the Bible is truly saying. You aren't reading the words as they appear in the original manuscripts.

One final approach is the functional equivalent approach, otherwise known as the paraphrase approach. As its name implies, this approach aims to paraphrase Scripture into the most readable and understandable form possible.[53] This approach emphasizes *readability* over *accuracy* and *clarity*. Bibles that follow this approach would never use the phrase "cleanliness of teeth." Sometimes, they wouldn't even use the word famine because it is too difficult to understand (at least they are, according to them). Instead, they translate the phrase this way: "You know, don't you, that I'm the one who emptied your pantries and cleaned out your cupboards, who left you hungry and standing in bread lines." As you can see, they want people to understand what's being communicated, but they do so by adding their own words. The pro of this approach is that the Bible becomes very readable. However, the absolute biggest con of this approach is that you aren't getting the words of Scripture at all. You're getting someone else's words. So it's not even like you're reading the Bible anymore. Today's two most common paraphrase versions are the Message Bible and the Passion Translation.

Let me just issue a warning here for us to be aware of when it comes to both the thought-for-thought translations and the paraphrased versions. The further you get away from the word-for-word approach, the further you get away from *translation* and more into *interpretation*.

This is dangerous because we need and want to know what the Bible *says*, not what someone else thinks it *means*. Do you see the difference there? Take for instance, Galatians 2:19. If you look at the Greek of Galatians 2 19, it literally says, "That

I might live for God." That's very simple. "That I might live for God." It's a very literal translation, but the passion translation, one of the paraphrased versions, says, "So that I can live for God in heaven's freedom." Well, what in the world does that mean? Why did the translators feel the need to include those words when those words do not appear in the Greek text at all? Well, it's because they're *interpreting* rather than *translating*. They are communicating what they think the text means rather than telling us what it *says*. This is a big problem because what ends up happening is you might disagree with the translator's interpretation. You don't want to hear what they think Scripture means. We need to hear what Scripture says. God's words are inspired (2 Tim 3:16); ours are not. So, it's best to know what the Bible says rather than what they think it means. You don't want to hear someone's interpretation. You need an accurate translation.

All this explains why we have so many different versions of the Bible out there today. It's because there are these three basic approaches to translation, and the Bible you're reading will fall into one of those approaches. So then we get back to our main question. Well, which version is best? I really can't say. I don't know if there is a single best, perfect English translation, despite what many people claim, because certain people will claim that a particular English translation is not only the best Bible out there, but the only one true Christians use. But understand this: No translation is perfect. The KJV utilizes outdated language and does not use the best manuscripts available today. The NASB is so wooden and literal that it's almost unreadable. While more readable, the ESV still kind of sounds like Yoda from Star Wars at certain points and uses weird word order in sentences. It kind of sounds like backward talk sometimes. The NIV and the CSB are too loose and drift away from the original words of Scripture. The NLT brings in too much of their own thoughts. The Message and Passion

Bibles are not even translations at all. I don't even know if we can consider them Bibles at this point.

For me personally, when I'm studying Scripture or when I'm preparing sermons, I always start with the original languages. Then, I primarily use an ESV, the English standard version. However, I think one of the best approaches when studying Scripture is to use a number of Bible translations together. If you want to know what the Bible says and what the words of Scripture are, use an ESV, a NASB, a King James, or a New King James. If you want help understanding what the Bible means, then consult an NIV or a CSB. I can't recommend any paraphrased version, such as the Message or Passion Translation. Give preference to the word-for-word translations, but definitely use the thought-for-thought translations as you study. Also, Study Bibles can be really helpful when you're wanting to understand what you're reading. I guess if I'm pressed for an answer, my final recommendation would be to pick up an ESV. I'm not saying that it's the absolute best English translation available, but as someone who reads the original Aramaic, Hebrew, and Greek on a weekly basis, I can tell you that the ESV does seem to be the best combination of *accuracy* and *readability* that I have found so far.

So, I don't know that we can say which Bible translation is best, but I hope that my trying to answer this question has helped you some. I hope you understand, one, why we have so many different translations available today, and two, the approaches behind those translations so that you know how to pick one best suited for you. Regardless of which one you pick, get in the Word, dig into it, read it every day, and grow in your knowledge and understanding of what the Lord says and who He is, and grow in your wonder of God's grace in Jesus Christ.

Chapter 20

Is Satan's Real Name Lucifer?

✝

What do you think? How would many of you answer this question? Would you say yes? Would you say no? Or would you say, I don't know? Maybe you say, I don't know. That's the reason I submitted the question. So just get on answering it. And I am, I'm going to. But fun fact: as we start, did you know that there's not one single place in all of Scripture where Satan is called lucifer? It's true. You can do the research for yourself. So the question is, how did the word lucifer come to be associated with Satan? Well, you can thank a guy named Jerome for that.

Jerome, also known as Saint Jerome, was a Christian priest, theologian, and historian who lived in the fourth and fifth centuries AD. He's best known for his work in translating the Bible into Latin, which became known as the Latin Vulgate. Jerome's translation was highly influential and became the standard version of the Bible for the Western Church for many centuries. Okay, so what does this have to do with Satan and the word lucifer? Well, we're getting to that. Just give me a second, okay? You see, the only place in all of Scripture where our English Bibles use the word lucifer is in Isaiah 14:12 and only in the King James Version and the New King James Version. In other English translations, Isaiah 14:12 reads, "How you were fallen from heaven, O day star, son of dawn, How you are cut down to the ground, You who laid the nations low."

Now, the important phrase in that verse is, "O day star, son of dawn." In the original Hebrew, the phrase is, *helel ben shahar.* In Hebrew, *helal* literally means "morning star" or "day star." However, in the King James Version and in the New King James Version, Isaiah 14:12 reads, "How art thou fallen from heaven, O Lucifer, son of the morning, How art thou cut down to the ground, Which didst weaken the nations." In those versions, the word lucifer is capitalized, indicating that it's a proper noun, probably because Isaiah 14 is a taunt against the King of Babylon. The word "lucifer" comes directly from the Latin Vulgate. In Latin, the word lucifer literally means "light-bearer" or "morning star."[54] It was actually a reference to the planet Venus, which was visible early in the morning.[55] So when Jerome was translating the Hebrew Bible into Latin and came across the word *helel*, he knew that it meant "morning star."

So, what do you do if you're translating from Hebrew into Latin and you come across a phrase or a word that means "morning star"? Well, you find the appropriate Latin word that means "morning star," which in this case is "*lucifer.*" Jerome made sure not to capitalize the word because he knew that it was not a proper noun. However, the early English translations didn't follow him on that. The early English translations of the Bible did begin to capitalize the word, and since many people believe that Isaiah 14 is about the fall of Satan, people began to believe that Satan's real name is Lucifer.

I'm also aware of the fact that there is a show on TV right now called Lucifer. I've never seen it, but it's my understanding that the main character's name is Lucifer Morning Star. Two comments are worth making on this. One, making a TV show idolizing the enemy of God is a horrible and despicable idea. No Christian should be watching that show. You should never have anything to do with something that is going to idolize the enemy of God. But two, it's hilarious that the TV show and the producers did not even do the basic research to see how wrong and redundant that name is. It's wrong because Satan's name is not Lucifer, and it's hilariously redundant because the name Lucifer Morning Star literally means Morning Star Morning Star. They didn't even do the research necessary to figure that out. So that's how the word Lucifer came to be associated with Satan. That's why many people think that Satan's real name is Lucifer, but it's not. It's just the Latin translation of the Hebrew word for Morning Star. You will find absolutely no place in all of Scripture that ever refers to Satan as Lucifer because that's not his name. It's just the result of what happened when they decided to capitalize a word that is not a proper noun, and now it's become associated with Satan ever since then.

Chapter 21

Do People Who Commit Suicide Go to Heaven?

✝

That's a good question, but I also understand that that's a really sensitive topic. All of our questions are submitted anonymously, so I don't know who submitted this or what that person is going through personally. I'm unsure if they're just curious or if someone they know is struggling with suicidal thoughts. I don't know the situation, but I do recognize that this is a sensitive issue, so we will handle it with care. The full question is actually this: What does the word say about suicide? What is God's stance on suicide? Do those who commit suicide go to heaven, or do they automatically go to hell? Since this is such a sensitive issue, you don't need Alex's opinion on this. We need to know what the Bible says about this issue. So let's dive in and let's see what the Word of God says about suicide.

As we open the Bible, we find that it actually doesn't really address the issue of suicide directly, at least in terms of those questions that were asked. There are about six people in Scripture who committed suicide: Abimelech in Judges 9:54, Saul in 1 Samuel 31:4, Saul's armor bearer in 1 Samuel 31:4-6, Ahithophel in 2 Samuel 17:23, Zimri in 1 Kings 16:18, and Judas in Matthew 27:5. In each of these cases, the Bible simply records the fact that these people took their own lives but doesn't really make any comments about the morality of the actions taken. In other words, it's more of just recording the history that has happened rather than offering some sort of statement about their decisions to do such a thing. However, just because Scripture doesn't really address suicide directly doesn't mean that it's not addressed at all.

For instance, Scripture lets us know that suicide is a sin. Suicide is a sin, according to the Bible, because it's a form of murder. It is self-murder. God says in Exodus 20:16, "You shall not murder." So, since suicide is a form of murder, self-murder, it is a sin in the eyes of God.

That being said, let's address and clear a few things up. Nothing in Scripture indicates that suicide is a worse sin than any other sin. What I don't want to happen is I don't want people to hear me say, "Suicide is a sin," and think that I'm automatically condemning someone to hell. That's not what I'm doing. The Bible does not indicate that suicide is worse than any other sin. It just makes clear that suicide is a sin because it is a form of murder.

However, for some reason, many people today seem to be unclear on that. Suicide is such a complicated issue that we do have people wondering things like, well, do people who commit suicide go straight to hell? They're not sure if the nature of the sin is greater than others and would, therefore, necessitate harsher punishment. I think this is one of the big issues that we have with suicide, is we know that it is a devastating sin. We know it is a tragedy, affecting so many different people. We know that it's a serious sin, so we ask those types of questions like, well, does this mean that that person is automatically going to hell because they've done such a thing?

Again, let's be clear that there is no reason to believe that according to Scripture. We need to clarify some confusion here and understand that suicide is not the determining factor of where you spend eternity. All right. Let's just say that again for anybody who's really needing to hear that. Suicide is not the determining factor for where someone spends eternity. Even though suicide is a sin, it's important to remember that it is not the determining factor of whether or not someone goes to heaven or goes to hell because the Bible teaches that the only way to go to heaven is to repent of your sins and trust in Christ alone for your salvation. The Bible also teaches that anyone who refuses to repent of their sins and trust in Christ will go to hell. So, suicide is not what sends people to hell or keeps people out of heaven. Faith in Christ is the sole determining factor of where you will spend eternity.

Now, with that said, there is another important question that is asked here, and that is, "Would true Christians ever commit suicide?" Yes, that's entirely in the realm of possibility. Countless Christians throughout history have struggled with depression. Some of the greatest Christians who have ever lived have battled ongoing depression for years. Many of them battled depression for most of their lives. The great prince of preachers, Charles Spurgeon, struggled with depression. The prophet Jeremiah struggled with what looked like depression in the Bible. Martin Luther also struggled with depression a great deal, and I can list many others, like Adoniram Judson and countless other Christians. All of this is to say that many Christians throughout their lives have struggled with their mental health and depression. Many Christians have not only struggled with depression but also suicidal thoughts. Just to be completely open with you, this has been part of my story.

For the better part of my life, I have struggled with ongoing depression, and at many different points, I have struggled with suicidal thoughts. For those who know my testimony, you know that the Lord saved me when I was literally about to kill myself. I was in the process of taking my own life when the Lord intervened and saved me. And if I'm honest with you, I've struggled with deep depression and suicidal thoughts ever since that time. In other words, they didn't just go away and never return simply because I was a Christian. This has been an ongoing battle for me, and the same is true for a lot of other Christians.

The other thing that we need to consider alongside the suicide issue is not just the reality of declining mental health in our country and around the world. It's not even just the reality of depression amongst Christians and things like that. More than all that, we always have to remember that we have an enemy. We have an enemy who wants us to sin and would love nothing more than for us to usurp God's authority over our lives and fail to trust Him by taking our own lives. We have to remember that God alone is the authority over our lives. He brought us into this world, and we will leave it when it's His will for us to leave it. We don't have the right to end our lives; only God does. Satan wants us not to trust God and not to depend on God. He wants us to take authority back over our own lives and determine for ourselves when we can end our lives, what we can do with our lives, and how we live our lives. He wants nothing more than to get us to rebel against God, and taking our own lives is an act of defiance against the authority of God and the authority that God has over our lives.

We need to understand something, folks, and you know this already. Life is hard. Not just for unbelievers, life is hard, especially for Christians. There are times when it feels like we're just barely making it. Like we're drowning and trying to stay afloat. Like we're suffocating, and we're unable to get a breath.

When we feel like we can't possibly keep on living, and we feel like we've lost all our strength and we're lost, and we feel hopeless, we need to remember that in those times, we are called to trust God. He is our rock, fortress, strength, and preserver; He alone upholds us and sustains us. We are to rely on Him and His power to keep us going rather than giving in to the darkness and allowing it to overcome us, so while it is possible for a true Christian to end up taking his own life, it would be incredibly rare for that to happen because number one, a true Christian would not want to sin against God willingly, and suicide is a sin. Number two, a true Christian would not want to usurp God's authority over life and death by taking his own life. Number three, a true Christian would not want to give in to the enemy and believe the enemy over God and His ability to see us through every difficult time and trial.

That's what we need to know about suicide. It is a sin, but please understand it's not the thing that keeps a person out of heaven or sends a person to hell. Our eternal destinies are determined by salvation in Christ alone. It is possible that a true Christian could commit suicide, but I do think it would be incredibly rare. Finally, suicidal thoughts and tendencies are a real struggle for many people today, whether Christians or not. I'm not trying to deny or downplay those struggles at all because I'm all too familiar with them. They still hit me from time to time. However, I want to encourage you to surround yourself with people who will love you and invest in you. One of the best things you can do is get plugged into a local church, join a small group, connect with other Christians, and then listen to me. This is the most important part: You've got to be willing to open up to them.

No one can help you if no one knows what's going on. It's hard to take that first step and go to someone and tell them what you're struggling with. It's hard to take that first step and go to someone and tell them how you're feeling and that you are having suicidal thoughts and you don't really have the desire to keep on living. I know what a struggle that is, but listen to me: you have to open up to someone because no one can help you if no one knows what's going on. There's a lot of stigma around mental health in the church today, but I'm a big proponent of taking care of and prioritizing your mental health. If you're struggling with depression or suicidal thoughts, you need to tell someone. You need to open up to them, and you need to let them help you. Most of all, folks, you need to take it to the Lord in prayer. The Bible tells us to cast all our cares upon him because he cares for us (reference the passage). That applies to you, too, Christian. He cares for you. So take your cares to Him.

Chapter 22

Does Science Point
Us to God?

✝

We had a similar question recently. That question was, has science disproven God? Which was also really fun, but the question is, does science actually point us to God? The answer to that question is yes, science does point us to God. It actually does so in a number of different ways. The one that we're going to be talking about in this chapter goes by different names. Sometimes, you'll hear it referred to as the anthropic principle. Other times, you'll hear this referred to as the teleological argument for God. Both essentially refer to the same thing: that our universe seems specifically tailor-made and designed for us.

Anthropic comes from the Greek word for man, which is anthropos.[56] Teleological comes from the Greek word telos, which refers to something's end purpose or design.[57] So these are just saying that our world seems to have been designed for mankind. Now I know that if a non-Christian hears me say that, they're going to dismiss me, thinking quickly, well, of course, you would think that; you're a Christian, so you believe that God created everything and that God designed everything. I do believe that, but non-Christian scientists also recognize the fine-tuning of our universe.

Consider this quote from the late Stephen Hawking, an atheist, physicist, and professor, "Our universe and its lulls appear to have a design that is both tailor-made to support us and, if we are to exist, leaves little room for alteration that is not easily explained and raises the natural question of why it is that way... The discovery, relatively recently, of the extreme fine-tuning of so many of the laws of nature could lead at least some of us back to the old idea that this grand design is the work of some grand designer."[58] Of course, he is right. In fact, British physicist Paul Davies has also marveled at the extreme fine-tuning of the universe, saying, "The really amazing thing is not that life on earth is balanced on a knife-edge, but that the entire universe is balanced on a knife-edge, and would be in total chaos if any of the natural 'constants' were off even slightly."[59] So, let's get into some of these examples of the extreme fine-tuning of our universe and see how science points us to God.

Our first example is that of hydrogen. "If the strong nuclear force were only slightly more powerful, then there would be no hydrogen, an essential element of life. If it were only slightly weaker, then hydrogen would be the only element in existence."[60] Not only that, but we have an example of the electromagnetic force. "If the electromagnetic force were slightly stronger or weaker, atomic bonds and complex molecules could not form."[61]

We have plenty of other examples, too. You have an example of the strength of gravity. Physicists say that if the strength of gravity were different by just one part in 10 to the 60th power, there could be no stars and galaxies. A tiny bit stronger, and all the matter would have collapsed back in on itself. A tiny bit weaker, and the matter would have spread out too quickly for anything like galaxies or stars to be able to form.[62] Of course, we need those things if we're to have planets, specifically planets that we would live on.

I mean, we can even get down to the atoms themselves. Every atom has a nucleus of protons and neutrons and a cloud of electrons swirling around it. When an atom binds with another atom to make a molecule, the charged protons and electrons interact to hold them together. Now, here's the important bit. The mass of a proton is nearly 2000 times the mass of an electron, but if this ratio changed by only a small amount, the stability of many common chemicals would be compromised. In the end, this would prevent the formation of many molecules, listen, including DNA, the building blocks of life. So if this proton to electron mass ratio was different by even the slightest bit, we could not have DNA.[63]

We can even look at many examples from our own earth, which is amazing. Earth's magnetic field, for instance, if it were any weaker, our planet would be devastated by cosmic radiation. If it were any stronger, we would be devastated by severe electromagnetic storms.[64] Then there's also the tilt of the earth. You all know from looking at a globe that the earth is tilted, and the axial tilt ensures not only an optimal temperature but that the temperature will be normalized over the planet's surface. If the rotational period of the earth were any longer, the difference in temperature between night and day would be too drastic. If it were any shorter, the atmospheric wind would be too fast.[65]

Then, you can even look at the earth's gravity. If the earth's gravity were any stronger, the atmosphere would retain too much ammonia and methane. If it were any weaker, it would lose too much water.[66] We can move even beyond our own earth and look to the solar system. If our sun were redder or bluer, plants would not be able to use sunlight for photosynthesis, which is essential. The sun's magnetic field is perfectly aligned to protect us from cosmic rays yet not generate too high of an X-ray flux.[67]

You can even think about the position and sizes of the gas giant planets that are in our solar system. They are imperative that they have to be where they currently are. If they were closer or larger, they would catastrophically affect Earth's orbit around the sun. If they were smaller or farther away, they wouldn't cause as many comets and asteroids to detour away from the interior of the solar system.[68] In fact, you can research this and see how many comets and asteroids Jupiter, in particular, takes that if it didn't get hit by those, those comets and asteroids would actually hit the earth. It's actually pretty amazing when you start to do the research and see all these comets that would be hitting us, but because of Jupiter's huge gravitational pull, they hit Jupiter instead. So we should all be wearing t-shirts that say, thank God for Jupiter. So these are just a few pretty compelling examples of the fine-tuning of our universe.

You can research all the examples I've listed here. You can even research more examples for yourself because there are a ton of them. But at the end of the day, we have to go another step further and ask, well, why is our universe so finely tuned? That's the question that everybody has to deal with. When you realize that our earth, our universe, is finely tuned, you have to ask, why is it like that? This is a huge problem for atheist scientists because every atheist scientist understands the problem of fine-tuning the universe.

That's why like I read before from Dr. Stephen Hawking, he said that "it appears that our universe has been tailor-made for us." Even he acknowledged that he could understand why fine-tuning would send many people back to God. It's why the atheist scientist Richard Dawkins has conceded that our universe is fine-tuned but dismisses it as saying it merely appears to be designed. He says it's not actually designed. It just has the appearance of design. So please understand what I'm saying here. No one, whether Christian, scientist, atheist, or anything in between, denies the reality that our universe is incredibly fine-tuned. The question is, why is it like that?

There really are only three possibilities. The first possibility that many atheists went with for a long time was the answer that our universe is this way because of chance accident or evolution. This is just what we got through the evolutionary process. However, blind, unguided accidents that occur within the theory of evolution cannot explain the high levels of fine-tuning that we have today. Even atheist scientists today recognize the complete improbability of this level of fine-tuning happening by chance. The odds are actually incalculable, making it impossible, which is why many scientists have abandoned the idea that our universe ended up this way due to chance.

Therefore, they've moved on to their next theory, which has become their favorite theory and a mainline idea within the scientific community today. It's the idea of the multiverse. That's right. The multiverse is not just for Marvel movies. It has actually become a mainline scientific theory. In fact, it's really interesting. If you research the formation of the multiverse hypothesis, one of the main reasons for its proposal is the fine-tuning of our universe. Scientists can't explain it by chance and don't want to mention God. So they propose a multiverse because if there are an infinite number of possible universes, then one of those universes will have all of the finely-tuned attributes that ours has, which allows for life to be possible. So, that is now their favorite explanation. They say, okay, we can't explain it by chance. We don't want to invoke God. So what if there is a multiverse in which an infinite number of possibilities, actually every single possibility that could exist, does exist? That would explain how we have a universe with everything we need for life to be possible.

The multiverse actually solves a number of problems for scientists. It helps explain how our universe even began to exist, which we covered in an earlier question, which, if you'll remember, scientists have absolutely no explanation for. The multiverse also helps explain the high fine-tuning levels that exist within our universe. So, I don't want you to overlook this or miss what I'm saying here. I'm literally telling you that one of the main reasons we are hearing scientists talk about a multiverse today is to avoid having to admit that without a multiverse, God is the best explanation of our universe. I'm personally amazed that the multiverse is even a legitimate theory today, considering the fact that it is so unscientific.

For instance, there's literally no way to test the multiverse theory, which, if I remember correctly from science class, being able to test something is key to the scientific process. You come up with a hypothesis, you're able to test that hypothesis, and then you need to be able to recreate it and reproduce the results. If you can't do those things, you have no legitimate theory. And yet, the whole multiverse theory it can be theorized, but it cannot be tested in any way.

You see, it's actually kind of funny and ironic because scientists used to accuse Christians and still accuse Christians of this thing called God of the gaps. Maybe you've heard of it. Basically, it was anytime science couldn't come up with an answer for something, Christians would say God is the answer. You know, why is there something rather than nothing? Science can't answer that. So we say, well, God, God created everything. In the beginning, God created the heavens and the earth. Science looks at our fine-tuned universe, and they say, well, we can't explain it. We say, oh, we can, God did it. So they would just say, well, you just put God anywhere where we haven't found a scientific theory to explain this thing we're looking at. It's a God of the gaps. What's funny and ironic is that they're now falling into the same problem with the multiverse. It's a multiverse of the gaps. Anytime science now can't explain anything, they just explain it away with the multiverse, even though there's absolutely no way to explain or explore such a theory. So, how do we have something rather than nothing? The multiverse. How do we have a universe that's so finely tuned? A multiverse. Anytime they can't explain something, and they don't want to invoke God, they just explain it away with the multiverse.

However, I did say there were three possibilities. You have chance, you have multiverse, and then the final explanation for fine-tuning, which I do think is the best explanation: God. God is the best explanation for why our universe is so finely tuned that it cannot be altered even slightly and still allow for life as we know it to be possible. When you see such a design, how can you not conclude that it is a designer?

For instance, if you were walking in a jungle next to a stream and you notice that in the stream, rocks were placed in such a way that they redirected the water flow to an eddy off to the side. And you looked, and you saw fish trapped in that eddy. Then you looked further, and you noticed that at the bottom of that eddy, there were some tree prawns woven in such a way that they could be picked up to collect fish. Now, that would be amazing. If you're just walking in the jungle and you see such a thing, that would be amazing. But you would never stop and say, this is amazing. I can't believe these rocks just happened to be placed in such a way that they send fish directly to that eddy and that some tree prawns just happened to be woven in such a way and placed in such a way that anyone can capture fish anytime they need them. What an amazing coincidence. What an amazing accident. No one would ever say that.

If you were walking in that jungle and you saw that in that stream, you would immediately recognize that such designs require a designer. You would know immediately that someone had specifically designed this fish trap so that they could collect fish from the stream. In the same way, when you look at our universe and its intricate design, the only legitimate solution is that it had a designer. All designs have a designer, and God is the best explanation for the very evident design of our universe.

So yes, science does point us to God in many ways. One of the best ways it points us to God is in its incredible design and the fact that it is so finely tuned that nothing can be altered. So, I encourage you to go and research this for yourself. You can look up the anthropic principle, the teleological argument for God, or even the fine-tuning of the universe. You will be amazed at how finely tuned our universe is and how it points us to God. Also, I just want you to remember that God created science, so science will never disprove God. Instead, it actually points us to God. So thank you for the question. I really appreciate that question. It's always fun getting to talk about science and God, and I look forward to answering more in the future.

Chapter 23

Is David and Goliath About Facing Our Giants?

✝

There are a lot of bad interpretations of this story. It's one of the most popular stories in the entire Bible, and yet it is often one of the most misunderstood, misinterpreted, and misapplied stories in the entire Bible. The way this story is typically preached today and taught in Sunday school or in devotionals is that you can overcome the giants in your life. That is, just as David defeated Goliath, so too you can face and overcome whatever your giants are, whether they are depression or anxiety, a bad boss, financial hardships, medical problems, or addiction, whatever your giant is, you can overcome it just as David overcame Goliath. However, I really just want to say at the start that while you can overcome the problems you face through God's grace and enabling power, that is not what this story is about. I would go so far as to say that none of those are even appropriate applications of this story. This story is about

Jesus, plain and simple. David serves as a shadow or a picture of Jesus and His triumph over Satan.

You see, we have a pretty big problem in the church today of eisegesis. Eisegesis, if you're unfamiliar with that word, it simply means reading something into the text that's not there. So with stories like this, we typically try to read ourselves into the story and ask, okay, who am I in this story? Let's be honest; most of the time, we make ourselves out to be the hero, don't we? We read this story and say, okay, I'm clearly David; my problems are Goliath, and God will give me the power to overcome all of my problems just as He gave David the power to overcome Goliath.

That's typically how we read this story and think about this story, but please understand me on this; if we are anyone in this story, we're the scared Israelites cowering in fear, doing absolutely nothing while our enemy taunts us. Rather than committing eisegesis, we need to commit ourselves to exegesis instead. If you aren't familiar with that word, exegesis simply means drawing out what is there from the text. So, rather than reading ourselves into the story, we want to draw out what is there rather than reading something into the story that's not there. As I said before, this story is all about Jesus. I say that now I have to prove it. So, let's dive in. Let's see how this story is about Jesus.

The story of David and Goliath occurs in 1 Samuel 17. but we can't just start there. That's like the middle of the biblical story, right? You would never pick up a book and just start reading in the middle of that book because you'd be totally lost as to what's going on. You wouldn't even know who the characters are, the storyline, or anything like that. In the same way, when we read stories like this in the Bible, we have to keep in mind the bigger biblical picture, the bigger biblical story that's going on. Let's remember all the way back to Genesis.

Adam and Eve rebelled against God. In chapter 3, God pronounces the punishment for their sin and rebellion. Women will have increased pain in childbirth and desire to usurp the husband's God-given role. Men will have to work hard in order to provide. Creation itself is even affected by our sin. It only yields fruit after much hard labor and often produces thistles and weeds. God also pronounces a curse upon the snake who tempted Adam and Eve into sin in the first place. God says the snake will be the lowest of all creatures and will have to slither around on its belly. However, in the midst of those punishments, God also pronounces a promise. He gives the people, gives us, gives Adam and Eve a promise in Genesis 3:15. He says, "I will put enmity between you and the woman and between your offspring and her offspring. He shall bruise or crush your head and you shall bruise his heel." It's a promise that one day, there's going to be an offspring of the woman who would crush the head of the snake and bring about a total reversal of sin's curse and bring renewal to God's creation. God gives us glimpses of this promise coming to fruition throughout Scripture.

For instance, we see a shadow of this promise in the person of Moses. You'll remember Moses was a deliverer. He was going to deliver God's people from an oppressor, and that oppressor was Pharaoh. Interesting thing about Pharaoh, by the way, and you can see this often in TV shows, movies, and pictures depicting a Pharaoh. The Pharaohs of Egypt wore a diadem, and in the very middle of that diadem was a snake.[69] So, in Moses versus Pharaoh, you have a son of a woman versus a snake. You'll remember that God had Moses tell Aaron to throw down his staff and that staff became a snake (Exodus 7:8-13). Then Pharaoh had his magicians conjure up snakes as well, but Aaron's snake *consumed* (Hebrew= *bala*) those snakes. They were defeated (Exodus 7:8-13). Eventually, Moses led the people of Israel out from under the oppression of the snake, but Pharaoh chased them through the parted waters of the Red Sea. Those waters, you'll remember, closed up on Pharaoh and all the Egyptians who were pursuing them, and the Bible says that Pharaoh was *swallowed up* (Hebrew= *bala*). Interestingly, the phrase "swallowed up" is the same word for "swallowed" that occurred when Aaron's snake *consumed* Pharaoh's snakes. The connections are easy to miss in English, but they are also incredibly important for understanding the bigger biblical picture being painted: What you have in Moses versus Pharaoh is a picture, a foreshadowing, of a son of a woman delivering God's people from the oppression of a snake.

So then that takes us all the way back to David and Goliath. Before their fight begins, at this point, the prophet Samuel had already anointed David as the new king of Israel. The Spirit of God comes upon David, so he has the Spirit and the anointing of God. However, he doesn't assume the throne just yet, but he is God's man. He is God's anointed new king over Israel. The king of Israel was supposed to lead God's people, protect God's people, and imitate God. At this point in Israel's history, they are at war with the Philistines. We're finally introduced in chapter 17 to the champion of the Philistines, Goliath. In chapter 17:4-7, we have a very long description of Goliath's appearance. How tall he is, what kind of armor he's wearing, all that kind of stuff. A whole long section just shows how well-armored he is, which contrasts how much armor and protection he has, as opposed to David, who will ultimately face him without any armor (reference). Verse 5 is the really interesting verse because this is what the Bible says in 1st Samuel 17:5, describing Goliath: "He had a helmet of bronze on his head, and he was armed with a coat of mail and the weight of the coat was 5,000 shekels of bronze."

Now, our English Bibles do us a great disservice here. A huge swing and a miss here. It's such a vital and important point in Scripture, but it mistranslates something here that it should have translated literally because there's a whole lot of biblical theology going on that's needed. You see, that phrase, "coat of mail," is the important phrase. The word that our English translations translate as "mail" is actually "*qaśqeśet*," the Hebrew word for *scales*.[70] It was the word that was used to describe how fish looked because, obviously, fish have scales, but more importantly, it was the word used to describe *the appearance of snakes*. Snakes were covered in this particular Hebrew word, meaning scales. So the Bible is saying here if you were to look at Goliath, he was covered in an armor of scales. In other words, you look at Goliath, and he looks like a what? A giant snake.

But it gets even better. This is why the Bible is so cool. Do you remember how David actually killed Goliath? 1 Samuel 17:49 says, "And David put his hand in his bag and took out a stone and slung it and struck the Philistine on his forehead. The stone sank into his forehead and he fell on his face to the ground." Now, I'm all about repeated words in the Bible, and I want you to notice that three times in this one verse, it mentions the *head*. You have the forehead mentioned twice and the face mentioned once. So why all this focus on the head? Well, now that we've done our background on the passage, we know it goes all the way back to the promise in Genesis 3:15, the promise that a son of the woman would crush the *head* of the serpent.

We have yet another picture of a son of the woman crushing the head of what? Of a giant snake. David, anointed and empowered by the Spirit of God, literally crushes the head of an enemy of God who is dressed like a snake, and he does so by crushing his head. Ultimately, it's a picture of what Jesus would do during his earthly ministry. Jesus is the ultimate fulfillment of Genesis 3:15. He is the son of the woman who crushes the head of the snake, Satan. By doing so, He delivers God's people from the bondage of sin, death, and Satan. He undoes sin's curse, and He begins to bring about a renewal of God's creation back to its original design.

So, the story of David and Goliath is not at all about you facing and overcoming the giants in your lives. It's about how God is faithful to fulfill His promises. Ultimately, it points us to Jesus and His victory over sin, death, and Satan. Therefore, when this passage is taught, it needs to be said that our greatest enemies or our greatest giants are not our financial problems, not our anxieties, our stress, our bad bosses, our bad health, or anything else like that. Our biggest enemy is sin and that ancient serpent who is the devil. We are like the cowering Israelites, powerless to do anything at all about it. We need someone to go in our place and defeat them for us. And we get that with Jesus. Jesus literally goes out in our place to face our enemy, and He crushes the head of the serpent and wins the battle for us. It's all about Jesus.

So, I really do appreciate the question. I hope that this has been helpful. I hope you understand now that this passage isn't about you facing your giants, but I also hope you see the importance of digging into Scripture. I hope you understand that when you read stories like this, you can't lose sight of the bigger biblical story that's going on. You have to remember what God is doing. You have to remember redemptive history. I know that not everybody reads the original languages as I do, but it's always good to use some sort of Bible software or something and check the words out for yourself. I mean, you could go to a website called Blue Letter Bible. You can type in any verse, and it'll show you what the Hebrew and Greek words actually mean. You might be wondering, how would I have even known in the first place to look that up?

There are clues. For instance, when you're getting a long description of what a person looks like, especially like Goliath here, and you begin to see this long description of how he looks and the type of armor he's wearing, you have to stop and just ask questions. I always tell people to ask two more questions. When you're studying the Bible, just ask two more questions, and you begin to get more out of it than you thought you could have upon initial reading. So, just ask two more questions. Just say, okay, why is there such a long description here when no one else is getting a long description of how they're dressed? And is there something more significant going on here? When you do that, you begin to study the passage for yourself, type it into Blue Letter Bible, look at all the words for yourself, and realize that that word mail is scales. And when you see scales, and you realize what's going on here, you're immediately reminded of the bigger picture, that this is God once again showing us He has not forgotten His promise, that He is going to send a son of woman to crush the head of the snake and deliver His people from sin. So pick up a Bible, dig in deeply, and focus on Jesus.

Chapter 24

Should Christians Revere the Pope?

✝

Let's just go ahead and get some distinctions out of the way. Okay? First, let's clarify what this question is not asking. This question is not asking what I personally think of the Pope. That's another issue entirely. That's another question entirely. If you're interested in that question, you should submit it to the podcast, and I'd be happy to answer it. This question is not asking if we should respect the Pope or treat him with respect, which you definitely should if you're a Christian. This question is specifically asking if we as Christians should revere the Pope, consider him holy, and follow him. There's a lot of confusion around this issue, especially in the eyes of the world. If you were to ask most people in the world, who is the holiest person in all of Christianity? The majority of people are going to say the Pope. Somehow, the Pope has become to Christianity what Buddha is to Buddhism, what Muhammad is to Islam, or what the Dalai Lama is to the Tibetan people. So the question is, is that true? Is the Pope the holiest person in Christianity? Should we, as Christians, revere him, consider him holy, and follow him? Put very plainly, the answer is no, we shouldn't. Now, let me defend and explain that position. Okay? There are two basic reasons why we, as Christians, should not revere the Pope or follow the Pope.

First and foremost, the office of the Pope is entirely un-biblical. There is nothing in Scripture that calls for the office of the Pope. I know there is going to be pushback on this point from many Catholics, and an in-depth explanation goes beyond the scope of this work; however, we should note a few points of consideration. Throughout the New Testament, we find words like bishops, overseers, shepherds, elders, pastors, and pastor-shepherds. Those words all refer to the exact same office, the office of pastor. It refers to men who lead local con-gregations and proclaim to them the Word of God and edify them and shepherd them and care for them. We also find the office of deacon in the New Testament. That office specifically refers to servants within the church, men who are qualified, according to biblical qualifications, to meet and care for the physical needs of church members. So think about it like this. Pastors/elders are to attend to the spiritual needs of the church, as well as some physical needs, but so that they can focus primarily on the spiritual needs of the church, God has blessed the church with deacons to care for the physical needs of the church body. These are the two primary offices within the church, as laid out by Scripture. There are, of course, many spiritual gifts that are utilized within the church, but in terms of offices, those are the two primary offices.

In other words, the New Testament never once recognizes or calls for there to be an office of the Pope. Now, many Catholics in our world today would push back on that, and they would say that the Bible does call for a Pope. They would say there's a place in Scripture where you see the first Pope being ordained or given his office. It occurs in Matthew chapter 16:17-19. This is what the Bible says, "Jesus replied, blessed are you, Simon, son of Jonah, for this was not revealed to you by man, but by my Father in heaven. And I tell you that you are Peter, and on this rock I will build my church and the gates of hell or the gates of Hades will not overcome it. I will give you the keys of the kingdom of heaven. Whatever you bind on earth, it will be bound in heaven. And whatever you loose on earth, it will be loosed in heaven."

Now, a couple of things here. What is the rock that Jesus refers to here? He says, upon this rock, I will build my church. What is that rock? Many Catholics today say it's Peter because his name means rock...kind of. Actually, there are two different words for rock being used here. Peter's name in Greek literally means "a little stone," and the word rock that Jesus uses here means large rock or bedrock. It refers to a solid foundation. So Jesus isn't saying that He is building His church upon Peter (the little stone), but His church is built upon Peter's answer to Jesus's question, "Who do you say that I am?"

Remember, Jesus asked Peter that very question. He had said, "Who do the people say that the Son of Man is?" (Matthew 16:13). His disciples gave all sorts of answers. Jesus turns to them, and He says, "But who do you say that I am?" And Peter replies, "You are the Christ, the Son of the living God" (Matthew 16:16). So understand this, folks. The confession that Jesus is the Christ, the Son of the living God, is the bedrock, the foundation of our faith. It is the confession upon which Jesus builds His church. It's no surprise that He calls Simon "Peter" at this point because, upon that confession, Peter becomes a little rock joined to the bedrock, to the foundation. Actually, this is true of every single believer in Christ. Peter himself seems to have understood Jesus's words in this way because later in his very own letter in 1 Peter 2:5-7, he says, under the inspiration of the Holy Spirit, "You yourselves like living stones," notice that he's calling believers stones, "You yourselves like living stones are being built up as a spiritual house to be a holy priesthood, to offer spiritual sacrifices acceptable to God through Jesus Christ. For it stands in scripture, behold, I am laying in Zion a stone, a cornerstone chosen and precious, and whoever believes in him will not be put to shame. So the honor is for you who believe, but for those who do not believe the stone that the builders rejected has become the cornerstone."

In other words, what Peter's saying there is that Jesus is the foundation. He is the cornerstone, and all believers who profess faith in Him and actually repent of their sins and trust in Him alone become living stones and are joined to that foundation, to that bedrock, and they become a spiritual house for the Lord. However, Catholics will go further and say that Jesus specifically gave Peter the keys of the kingdom and that the Pope today can trace his office all the way back to Peter. So what happened is Jesus named Peter as the first Pope, in their opinion, and then Peter named his successor, and then that person named his successor, and then so on and so forth all the way to today so that the keys of the kingdom have never left the possession of the Pope. They go on and say that Jesus specifically gave Peter, the first Pope, the right to bind and loose on earth in such a way that it will be done in heaven.

Now, a couple of things on that. First, nobody in the early church viewed Peter in that way. Peter was the first bishop/pastor of the church in Rome, but his authority was limited to that one church. He was specifically over the church in Rome. He could not exercise authority over any other church, and to think that he had some special authority over all churches or that he was set apart or special in some way, well, that's easily contradicted by the fact that Paul, who was persecuting the church and then converted to faith in Christ, went to Peter and confronted Peter and called Peter to repent of his hypocrisy. You can read about that in the book of Galatians. It's very dangerous to view Peter in this way when no one else in the early church viewed Peter in this way.

Something else just in regard to that Scripture that we just read in Matthew. Just two chapters later, Jesus says to His disciples, not just to Peter this time, but to all of His disciples who are with Him, He says in Matthew 18:18, "Truly I say to you, whatever you bind on earth shall be bound in heaven, and whatever you loose on earth shall be loosed in heaven." So notice this: Jesus did not just give this right specifically and only to Peter, but to all of His followers acting according to His will and authority. Now, Catholics will typically respond to this point by saying that the disciples here represent an authoritative body within the church, much like priests, bishops, cardinals, etc. Since they represent an authoritative body, Jesus is not saying every single believer possesses the authority given here but only those who have positions of authority within the church. They are the ones who have the ability to bind and loose. However, at this point in Scripture, the disciples of Jesus do not hold positions of authority within local church communities. They possess the authority Jesus has entrusted to them as His followers, but their authority is not yet within the bounds of a local church. In other words, at this point, it is less likely that they represent authorities within a church (like priests, bishops, cardinals, etc.), and it is more likely that they represent your average, everyday Christ-follower. So know this, please: there is no biblical basis at all for a Pope. However, I did say at the beginning that we shouldn't revere the Pope and follow him for two reasons. I want to get into that second reason now.

This one is crucial. You see, what the Bible specifically says of the Holy Trinity, the Catholic Church says of the Pope. That is a huge problem. I want to show you what I mean. The Pope's main title is Pope. Of course, he has a lot of different titles, but he's known as the Pope. In Latin, Pope means papa or father.[71]

Well, in Matthew 23, Jesus addresses the religious leaders of Israel, the scribes, and the Pharisees, and He condemns them for their hypocrisy. He says constantly, "woe to you." At one point, He turns to the crowd, and He says in Matthew 23:9, "And call no man your father on earth, for you have one father who is in heaven." Now, Jesus was not saying that we cannot call our parent our father. That's not the point here. You always have to keep in mind the context. Remember the context here. He's specifically talking to the religious leaders of Israel. So the context is within the spiritual community, within the leadership of God's people, and He says within the leadership of God's people, what we would call today the church, call no man father, for you have one father who is in heaven. Well, that gets completely ignored today with millions upon millions of people who call the Pope "papa," meaning father. So what is said of our Holy Father who is in heaven, they say of the Pope.

Not only that, it gets worse. One of the Pope's other official titles is Supreme Pontiff of the Universal Church.[72] The word pontiff derives from pontifex and means bridge.[73] The Catholic Church claims that the Pope is the bridge of the church, the bridge between man and God. Well, hold on now. When I look in the Bible, I see that Jesus is the one and only bridge between God and man. Jesus says in John 14:6, "I am the way, the truth and the life and no one comes to the father, but by me." In other words, if you want to bridge the gap between God and man, the only way to do that is through Jesus, not through the Pope, but through Jesus alone. The Bible also says in 1 Timothy 2:5 that "there is one mediator between God and men, the man Jesus Christ." Again, notice that the bridge between us and God is Christ and Christ alone. So once again, what the Bible affirms of the son, the Catholic Church claims of the Pope, and it even gets worse.

One of the other official titles of the Pope is Vicar of Jesus Christ.[74] The word vicar means "in the place of," and we use a version of this word when we speak of Jesus's vicarious atonement. It means that Jesus died *in the place of* us. He died in our place. It is a vicarious atonement. So, the Catholic Church says that the Pope stands in the place of Christ. In other words, since Christ has ascended back to the Father, we now have the Pope in His place. But again, hold on a second because when I look to Scripture, I see that Jesus specifically says that the Holy Spirit is His vicar, the one He sends in His place.

Jesus says in John 16:7, "Nevertheless, I tell you the truth. It is to your advantage that I go away, for if I do not go away, the helper, the Holy Spirit, will not come. But if I go, I will send him to you." In other words, listen to what Jesus is saying here; He is saying it is to our advantage that He goes back to the Father so that we would have, in His place, not the Pope but the Holy Spirit. So please understand what is going on here. What the Bible specifically claims about the Father, the Son, and the Holy Spirit, the Catholic Church claims about the Pope.

Therefore, no, we, as Christians today, should not revere or follow the Pope first because there is absolutely no biblical basis at all for the office of the Pope, and second because the Catholic church claims for the Pope what is meant only for the Holy Trinity.

Chapter 25

What Does the Bible Say About the Rapture?

✝

Honestly, I think that's probably the best way to word that question too. What does *the Bible* say about the rapture? I emphasize that aspect of the question because the topic of the rapture is maybe the topic that has been most affected and influenced by popular culture. Of course, by pop culture, I don't mean culture as a whole, but specifically referring to books and movies. I would say probably 90% of Christians today believe what they believe about the rapture, not based entirely on what Scripture says, but on what tradition says, as well as books and movies. I think most of you know that there was a very popular series called *Left Behind,* and that one series has influenced the church's beliefs today more than probably anything else. The *Left Behind* series popularized the most common view of the rapture today. It's this idea that everybody's going to be going about their day when suddenly people are just going to disappear and leave behind their clothes. There's not going to be a warning. It'll just happen out of nowhere, and all the unbelievers get left behind. That's what that series told us. But the question is, "Is that what the Bible teaches us?"

We need to understand that this view of the rapture is associated with an eschatological position called Dispensationalism. Now, don't get intimidated by those words. If you don't know what they mean, that's okay. Eschatology is just the study of the end times. Dispensationalism is just one of a number of views of the end times, and it is the most popular and the most common view in the church today. It has been that way for the past hundred years or so, but, very importantly, it hasn't always been this way. The history of dispensationalism is actually pretty interesting. Dispensationalism is a premillennial eschatology, meaning they simply believe Christ will return before the millennium (pre-millennium = before the millennium). Interestingly, Historic Premillennialism is another version of Premillennialism that has been the predominant view throughout church history, while Dispensationalism only began in the 1830s.[75] It was created by a man named John Darby.[76]

Now, here's what makes that interesting and what should cause us to reflect with consideration: the most common view of the rapture and eschatology in the church today was completely unknown and unheard of and unbelieved by any Christian for the first 1830 years of the church. Now, does that make it wrong? No. Should it be a red flag? Yes. It should give us cause for concern and make us investigate further. So, here's the question. How did this brand new theology become the most popular eschatological view and overtake the church today?

That's pretty interesting, actually. Basically, what happened is Darby's students, he was a Scotsman, brought Dispensationalism to America, where some key figures picked it up. One key figure in particular is responsible for its widespread popularity and acceptance in America. In order to understand how that happened, we have to remember the historical context of America in the early 20th century.

The King James Version of the Bible has been the most commonly used Bible translation since the 17th century. Now, think back to the context of America in the early 1900s. We were coming out of the Civil War and rebuilding as a nation. Some people were pursuing higher education, but the majority of Americans were laborers and not very educated at all, but they wanted to know the Bible. They just needed a little help since they weren't very educated. So, in 1909, a new study Bible was published that would alter the course of American Christianity from that point forward.[77]

If you were an American living in the early 1900s and your translation of choice was the KJV, and you wanted to better understand the Bible, and you heard that a new King James study Bible was just released, do you think you would buy that Bible? Yeah, of course you would. That's exactly what happened. Countless Americans bought the Scofield Study Bible based on the text of the KJV. That study Bible was so popular and influential many people still own it today. When Scofield first encountered Darby's dispensationalism from the students who came over to America, he ate it up hook, line, and sinker. He loved it, ran with it, and went all in on dispensationalism. He would be the one to popularize it in America. But there was a big issue with the study Bible that he released: Scofield's footnotes were entirely his own thoughts and opinions rather than coming from a group of theologians and an editorial team.

So again, just think back to this historical situation. If you were a mostly uneducated laborer who just wanted to understand the Bible better, and you bought this study Bible, you were going to believe anything it said because you didn't know any better. That's exactly what happened. People continued to buy the Scofield Study Bible, they continued to read it, and they accepted all of Scofield's thoughts and opinions uncritically. They weren't questioning anything at all. Because of that, Dispensationalism spread like wildfire throughout America. It continued to grow in popularity, and ultimately, it found its way into the mainstream media and culture through the *Left Behind* books and, later, the movies. This view has actually become so popular and widely accepted that if you disagree with Dispensationalism, many people would call you a heretic and unorthodox for disagreeing with a brand new theology created in 1830 by a Scotsman and popularized in America in 1909 by Scofield. That's just mind-blowing to me.

I'm on board if you want to have a different eschatological view than I do, that's fine. I don't make that a hill to die on. We can disagree on eschatology. That is fine. I would never call someone a heretic for having a different eschatological view than I have. But I think we need to understand that you shouldn't be calling someone else a heretic if they don't hold to your brand-new theology created in 1830. I mean, you'd have to go back through the history of the church and call every single one of the church fathers, all of the people who came after the church fathers, Augustine, Luther, Calvin, Knox, and Zwingli, and all of the reformers, you'd have to call all of them heretics. You would basically have to look through the entire history of the church before 1830 and call all of those people heretics and unorthodox because they did not believe in this novel theology that had not even been created yet.

So, what exactly is the Dispensational view of the rapture? It's important to clarify that what Dispensationalists mean by the rapture is not what the other eschatological views mean by the rapture. When Dispensationalists refer to the rapture, they're referring to a kind of "secret rapture" in which Christ partly returns to earth, stops in the sky, and calls up the church to meet Him there.[78] They picture people, again, going about their daily lives when all of a sudden, people start disappearing, and it calls to mind the *Left Behind* movies where you see clothes left all over the place and people left behind because the church has been summoned up or raptured up. Also, it's known as a "secret rapture" because there is no warning or fanfare; it just happens by surprise, and people just disappear. So the question is, where does this idea come from?

Dispensationalists will often appeal to a number of biblical passages in order to justify this belief or prove this belief. The main one is found in 1 Thessalonians 4:13-18. This is what that passage says, "But we do not want you to be uninformed, brothers, about those who are asleep, that you may not grieve as others do who have no hope. For since we believe that Jesus is the Lord, and that Jesus died and rose again, even so, through Jesus, God will bring with him those who have fallen asleep. For this we declare to you by a word from the Lord, that we who are alive, who are left until the coming of the Lord, will not precede those who have fallen asleep. For the Lord himself will descend from heaven with a cry of command, with the voice of an archangel, and with the sound of the trumpet of God, and the dead in Christ will rise first. Then we who are alive, who are left, will be caught up together with them in the clouds to meet the Lord in the air. And so we will always be with the Lord. Therefore encourage one another with these words."

Now, the word rapture actually comes from this passage. Well, actually, it comes from this passage as it appears in the Latin Vulgate. The Latin word *rapere* is used here for the two words "caught up," where we're going to be caught up together with them in the clouds. *Rapere* means to seize.[79] Again, remember that when Dispensationalists read this passage, they imagine a secret rapture because Jesus will not return visibly for all to see, but instead, He will call up the church to meet Him in the sky. They also believe this rapture is imminent, meaning it could happen at any second. This mostly comes from 1 Corinthians 15:52, which talks about how we will be changed in a moment in the twinkling of an eye. Another very popular passage they appeal to is Matthew 24, which talks about two people being in a field, one being taken away, and one being left behind. They say that this is a picture of that rapture idea where people are going about their day, and one disappears, one's left behind. So those are some of the key passages that dispensationalists will use to prove their belief in this kind of rapture.

But I want to offer a critique of this view. First and foremost, no one, again, in the entire first 1830 years of the church held to this view of a secret, non-visible rapture. That doesn't necessarily make it wrong, but it should cause us to question it a lot. It should cause us to investigate it because I think if no one got it right for the first 1830 years of the church, it's hard to imagine we're going to get it right after that. Maybe it's possible, but it should cause a lot of red flags. Second, and more importantly, it doesn't align with the Bible's teaching on Christ's visible return.

Consider Revelation 1:7. The Bible says, "Behold, He is coming with the clouds, and every eye will see Him, even those who pierced Him, and all the tribes of the earth will wail on account of Him. Even so, amen." Now, that clearly teaches that when Jesus returns, every eye will see Him, so it will be a visible return. But notice it goes further. It also teaches us that all people on the earth will be *aware* of His coming because notice it says there that all the tribes of the earth will wail on account of Him. They will know what is happening. They will know that Jesus is returning. They realize in that moment that the gospel is true, that the Christians were right, that the Bible is true. They understand what's happening, and they wail on account of Him.

Even more than that, go back to the 1 Thessalonians chapter 4 passage that the dispensationalists use to prove their belief in their view of the rapture. In that passage, it said that at Jesus's return, "He will descend with a cry of command, with the voice of an archangel and the sound of the trumpet of God." Now, that seems like it would be pretty hard to miss, right? Again, think about the Left Behind movies if you've ever seen them or the books if you've ever read them. There is no fanfare. There is no warning. Someone's driving a plane, and all of a sudden, the captain's gone, and the plane's going down. There is no sound of anything. And yet, the Bible says Jesus will be visible, and all people will know what's happening, and there will be a loud cry of command, the voice of an archangel, and the sound of the trumpet of God. It's going to be a massive fanfare event.

Furthermore, Dispensationalism shifts the New Testament hope. You see, all throughout the New Testament, the writers of the New Testament are anticipating one event: the return of Christ. I mean, Paul writes about the return of Christ and all that comes with that return. John writes of it. The author of Hebrews writes of it. Peter writes of it. They're constantly trying to get us as Christians to remember that Christ is coming back. They want us to long for that return, anticipate it, and look forward to His return. I mean, the book of Revelation even ends with Jesus saying, "Surely I am coming soon." John responds and says, "Amen, come Lord Jesus" (Revelation 22:20). The New Testament sees the next great cosmic event not as a secret rapture but as the return of Christ. Our longing should not be to be raptured away from this earth but for Jesus to come and come quickly.

Another important critique that we have to make here is that rather than focusing on the Latin word *rapere*, we need to focus on the Greek word "coming" from the phrase "coming of the Lord" as found in 1 Thessalonians 4:15. The Greek word used there is *parousia*. Another important word found in the Greek text is *apantesis*, which comes from the phrase "meet the Lord" from 1 Thessalonians 4:17. According to F. F. Bruce,

"When a dignitary paid an official visit (parousia) to a city in Hellenistic times, the action of the leading citizens in going out to meet him and escort him back on the final stage of his journey was called the *apantesis*."[80] In other words, if people knew that a king was coming to their city, they would go out and meet that king before he ever got there. They'd go out to meet him, welcome him, and then they would escort him back to the city. That's the picture that's being painted here. The Bible is not saying that God will call up Christians to meet Him in the sky for Jesus to escort us back to heaven. Quite the opposite. The Bible says that when Jesus returns, He will make a stop, a short pause in the sky, as He calls up His people to come and greet Him and welcome Him, and then *we* will escort *Him* back to earth. That's exactly what that Greek is indicating there.

One final critique and something to think about here. What's interesting about that reference to Matthew 24, where one person is taken, and one person is left behind, is you always have to interpret that in light of Matthew 13. Matthew 13 obviously comes before Matthew 24, and Matthew 13 is the parable of the weeds and the wheat. You are probably very familiar with this parable. Remember that the master of a house sends his servants out to plant his fields, and it says that overnight, an enemy came and sowed in some weeds amongst his wheat. As they began to grow, the servants saw weeds in the midst of the wheat, and they said to the master, Master, did you not use good seed? He's like, well, of course, I did, but an enemy has come and sown against us. His servants say, okay, well, what should we do? Should we go and pick all the weeds out? Interestingly, the master says, no, let them both grow until the end, lest you accidentally pick some of the wheat as you're trying to get the weeds. He says, at the end, we are going to gather up all the weeds, and we will throw them into the fire to be burned. Jesus later explains that it's a reference to what's going to happen at the end, that when

Jesus returns, He's going to send His angels, and the angels are going to gather up all the unbelievers and cast them into the fire where there is weeping and gnashing of teeth.

Now, think about that for a second. Who were the ones being taken in that scenario? It's not the Christians. It's the unbelievers. The angels come, they gather the unbelievers, and the ones who are left behind are not the unbelievers. They're the Christians. Therefore, Matthew 24, in light of Matthew 13, refers to Christians who are left behind after unbelievers are gathered up and taken away.

So what does the Bible say about the rapture? Well, it teaches us that Jesus will return visibly for all to see and with great fanfare with the sound of trumpets and the voice of an archangel and the command of a loud voice. Everyone on earth is going to know what is happening. Believers will rejoice, but the nations who do not know Christ or love Christ and have not repented of their sins and trusted in Christ will wail on account of His coming. However, the Bible goes on to explain that Jesus will descend partway to earth. He will pause there in the sky where He's going to call up or rapture up His church to meet Him there. As the Greek phrase indicates, all believers with joy will go to meet Jesus, and they will welcome Him. Then, we will gladly escort Him back to earth as a king preparing to re-enter His kingdom.

So, no, we don't know when that's going to happen. Only God knows that, but the Bible doesn't indicate that people will just start disappearing and leaving behind their clothes. Every eye will see, and every ear will hear. As Christians, we look forward to this return, and we all say together, come Lord Jesus, come quickly.

Chapter 26

Should Christians Believe in Karma?

†

Karma is one of the most popular beliefs today in the world, regardless of religious affiliation. It seems like it's almost an intrinsic belief that most people hold to some sort of karmic belief system. Karma is an Eastern belief. It comes from Buddhism and Hinduism, and essentially, karma is the idea that how you live and treat others determines your quality of life.[81] Essentially, there are basically two ways this plays out. The first is in this life. If you are kind and generous and treat people well, then you'll have a good life now, and good things will happen to you now. Second, interestingly enough, both Buddhism and Hinduism teach that the merit you build up now in this life carries over into your next life after reincarnation. In other words, if you live a good life now, treat people well now, and do good things now, then you will have a favorable reincarnation and a good next life.[82] To summarize, karma is the basic idea that living well, treating others kindly, and doing good things will result in a good life now and in your future reincarnated life. So here's the question. What does the Bible say about this, and how can we interact with this idea biblically?

In the Bible, the closest thing to karma that we find is the idea of reaping and sowing. For instance, Galatians 6:7 says, "A man reaps what he sows." Now, on the surface, that does seem a little bit like karma, does it not? A man reaps what he sows. In other words, it seems to imply that if I sow good things, I will reap good things, but if I sow bad things, I will reap bad things. That sounds a lot like karma. Pretty much every reference to reaping and sowing in the Bible does sound like karma, but there's an important difference that we need to understand and need to learn to recognize. When the Bible speaks about reaping and sowing, it's speaking in terms of *general principles*, **not** *guaranteed promises*. All right, so let's make sure we understand that when the Bible speaks of reaping and sowing, it is talking in terms of general principles, not guaranteed promises.

In other words, in general, if you sow bad things, you will reap bad things. In general, if you sow good things, you will reap good things. Life experience teaches us that this principle is generally true. For instance, if a person is bent toward deception and crime and acts according to those tendencies, we can generally expect that he will suffer the consequences of those decisions. He's going to be punished. He's going to end up in jail or worse. Generally speaking, that is true. Similarly, if a person is loving and volunteers and helps others and gives to charities, generally, we can expect that person to be well-loved and appreciated. People are going to look at that person very favorably. Generally speaking, these things are true, but again, they are just that. They are general principles, not guaranteed promises.

For instance, we also know that the Bible acknowledges and laments the fact that very often in our world because it is a fallen world, the wicked prosper and the righteous suffer.

Ecclesiastes speaks of this very often. We read in Ecclesiastes 7:15, "In my vain life I have seen everything. There is a righteous man who perishes in his righteousness, and there is a wicked man who prolongs his life in his evil doing." In other words, the author of Ecclesiastes is saying, I've seen righteous people die young even though they are righteous, but I've seen wicked people live good, long, happy lives even though they are wicked, and it's not fair.

We see this idea often in the Bible. In Psalm 73:3-5, the Bible says, "For I was envious of the arrogant when I saw the prosperity of the wicked. For they had no pangs unto death. Their bodies are fat and sleek. They are not in trouble as others are. They are not stricken like the rest of mankind." The psalmist there is lamenting that even though he and others are righteous, he has seen that arrogant, wicked people have no problems until they die. They will often have long, happy lives, and then they go, and they're not able to live, and they're not stricken like the rest of mankind, and he's saying, this is the reality of the world we live in, and it's not fair. So these passages and others like them acknowledge and lament that in this fallen world, the wicked will prosper very often.

Not only that, we also know that the Bible acknowledges and laments the fact that the righteous will also suffer. We can look to Job, who the Bible describes as blameless and upright (Job 1:1), and we see how great his sufferings and losses were. We can look to Paul and the other Apostles, who all did good and sowed much good in the world but who all suffered greatly and, apart from John, died horrible, martyred deaths. Most of all, we can look to Jesus, who was literally perfect in every way and without sin, who only sowed good all the time, and yet He suffered greatly and died a horrible death upon the cross. If karma were true and real, then none of these things would happen. The righteous wouldn't suffer, the wicked wouldn't prosper, but they do, and we know it. We can look around our world, and we see it. It is clear. So karma is not a Christian belief. It is not supported by the Bible.

However, here's what I've found. We all want karma to be true, don't we? Well, only in certain situations. You see, I tell my church fairly often that while most Christians would not say that they believe in karma, there's a dark place in all of our hearts that desperately wants karma to be true, and we want to believe that it is. We can prove this, too. It's fairly easy. When Christians begin to suffer, we desperately want to cry and say, why is this happening? What did I do to deserve this? Do you hear the karma in there? We're essentially saying, I've been good. I've done everything right. This shouldn't be happening to me. I've done good. I deserve good.

Or just think about when bad things happen to Christians, and their lives are falling apart, and everything is barely holding on by a thread. They will often cry out to the Lord and say something like, Lord, I've been going to church. I've been reading my Bible. I've been praying. I've been doing everything you've asked of me. So why is this happening? Again, do you hear the karma in there? Our expectation, even as Christians, is that we will *receive good* if we have *been good*. What we're actually doing in those moments is we are revealing our desire for justice. We recognize that our world is fallen and broken, that we exist in a world where the wicked prosper and the righteous suffer. We know that it isn't right. We desperately want someone to come along and fix the brokenness of our world and make all things right.

Interestingly enough, though, you never really hear people mention karma when they know that they've done wrong and deserve bad things to happen to them, right? Isn't that kind of interesting? Only when bad stuff is happening to us, and we feel like we don't deserve it, we reveal our deep desire for karma. However, when we know that we've done something wrong and gotten away with it, you never hear anyone mention karma then. It's because we know that grace is greater than karma. The grace of God is too wonderful for words. The mercy of God is too precious for words. When God shows us mercy, He does not give us the punishment that we deserve for the wrongs that we have committed. When He shows us grace, He lavishes His riches upon us when we deserve the exact opposite. Mercy and grace are infinitely better than karma.

So, should Christians hold to a belief in karma? The answer is no. Because one, the Bible clearly reveals that karma is not true, and two, because common sense and life experience clearly reveal that karma is not true. Generally speaking, very often, people will reap what they sow. We also know that human sin caused the brokenness of our world. So now, very often, the wicked prosper, and the righteous suffer. Within every single person is a longing for justice, for the right thing to be done in every circumstance, and also a longing for mercy and grace, for the undeserving to receive something contrary to what they deserve. Listen to me; both of those desires are satisfied in God. He is the judge of all the earth who will do right and make all things right. He will not overlook even one sin but punish the evildoer. Praise be to the Lord that He also provides us with a Savior who is full of mercy and grace, who is ready to forgive, who is ready to take the punishment that we deserve for our sins and give us the reward that He earned in His righteous life. So those longings for justice, mercy, and grace ultimately find their satisfaction in Christ. So, no, you should not believe in karma. You should look to Jesus, who satisfies the justice that God demands and provides us with the mercy and grace we desperately need.

Chapter 27

According to the Bible, Can Women Be Pastors?

✝

This is a good question, and as you know, it's an incredibly relevant question because the topic of women pastors is one of the hot topics of our day. This one has the potential to be heated. It has the potential to be controversial. You know that I don't shy away from the controversial questions. All I do is answer the questions submitted to me, and that's what we're going to do with this question. So let me just say, at the start, it is not my intention to offend, demean, or hurt anyone's feelings. I'm simply going to answer the question that was asked, and I'm going to do so by looking at what the Bible says. So, I'm *not* going to be giving you Alex's opinion on this. I will be telling you what the Bible says on this issue. For those who might disagree with or be upset by the answer to this question, I want you to understand that I'm deriving my answer from the Bible, which is our ultimate authority. That's what we're going to to look at.

Before we can even look at the passages concerning whether or not women can be pastors, we have to understand that this issue ultimately comes down to who or what is our ultimate authority. Here's what I mean by that. Whether we're talking about this issue or another issue, our answer will reveal whether God is our ultimate authority or if we are our own ultimate authority. If the Bible says something, God says something because the Bible is the inerrant, infallible, inspired Word of God. I make this point because when you address controversial issues like this, people sometimes claim that was Paul's opinion or that's what Paul thought, but Paul's not God. I agree Paul is not God. But do you see the danger there with separating the inspired author from the one who is inspiring his writing? You cannot separate a biblical author from the voice of God if God truly is the one speaking through the biblical author. All of that is to say, when we read the words of Paul or Peter or John or any of the other biblical authors, we are reading the very words of God since God inspired them. So, no, it is not Paul's opinion or just what Paul thought. It's God's truth and rule for our lives.

Another reason I mention ultimate authority is because, very often, people will claim that God tells them to do things that go directly against His revealed Word. For instance, I know of a couple who went to speak to their pastor, and the husband told the pastor that they wanted to get a divorce. The pastor counseled them, telling them that the Bible prohibits divorce with only two extreme exceptions. Then the husband told the pastor, well, God told me it was okay for me to divorce my wife. God wants me to be happy. The pastor wisely responded and said, well, God tells us in His Word that He hates divorce and only allows for it in two extreme circumstances. So what am I to believe? What God has revealed to us clearly and plainly in His Word or what you claim God told you in private?

That was a great response by the pastor because God will never contradict Himself or do something that would go against His Word. It's important to keep that in mind throughout this discussion because very often, there will be women who say, I feel very strongly that God is calling me to preach. I know that God has called me to be a pastor, but if we look into Scripture and find that God's Word prohibits that very thing, then we are forced to say that those people are mistaken because God would never do something that goes against His Word. He would never contradict Himself. I'm not denying their feelings. They may feel a certain way, but just because they feel a certain way doesn't make it true. Our feelings *cannot* and *should not* be our ultimate authority. God is our ultimate authority, and what He says in His Word must guide and direct us in our lives. Every belief that we hold as Christians must derive from Scripture. That is God's Word to us. It is His infallible and inspired Word. So, we shouldn't create our own beliefs based on what the culture says, what the society says, or even what we feel; our beliefs must be rooted in Scripture. So, with that in mind, let's jump into what the Bible says about pastors.

The first passage to consider is in 1 Timothy 2:12-14. In this context, Paul is talking about regulations for the church, and this is what he says, "I do not permit a woman to teach or to exercise authority over a man. Rather, she is to remain quiet. For Adam was formed first, then Eve, and Adam was not deceived, but the woman was deceived and became a transgressor." Now, that passage again is Paul stating regulations for the church, and he clearly says that women are not to teach or exercise any authority over men. That immediately excludes them from the pastorate since pastors must both teach and exercise authority in the church.

One of the most common rebuttals at this point in this passage comes from the historical context. Those who do support women pastors will say, well, the reason that Paul prohibits

women from being pastors and teaching in this passage is because back then, women were not educated, so they wouldn't
have had the capabilities to teach and would have led people
astray since they were uneducated. However, they claim since
women are highly educated today, this principle is no longer
binding on us; therefore, women can be pastors today.

Now, that would be a very compelling case if that were, in
fact, Paul's reason for prohibiting women from the pastorate,
but that's not Paul's reason. How do we know that's not Paul's
reason? Well, it's very clear. Look again at what the verse says.
Paul does not say that women aren't to preach or exercise
authority over men because they aren't educated. He doesn't
say anything at all about education. He grounds his reasoning
all the way back in the beginning to God's creation. He says
Adam was created first, meaning God created men first and
ordered creation in such a way that men are to be the leaders
of their families and leaders in the church. They are the ones
who carry the burden and the responsibility of leadership.

But then notice what Paul also says. He says the other
reason is that the woman was deceived, not the man. In other
words, when Eve assumed a role and a position that was never
meant for her, she fell into sin, led others into sin, and plunged
the world into sin. So Paul says absolutely nothing here about
women lacking education as being the reason they're not per-
mitted to be pastors. He grounds everything in God's ordering
of humanity and creation. God made men to be leaders in their
families and in the church, and when women assume those
roles and the order is reversed, you end up with disorder and
chaos.

Another reason the education argument doesn't hold up
is because of the Book of Acts. In the Book of Acts, when
Peter and John were preaching Jesus, it says that the crowds
marveled at them, as Acts 4.13 says, because they were uneducated, common men. Now, notice that. The Bible clearly says

that both Peter and John were uneducated, but God called both men to become pastors. Peter became the pastor of the church in Rome, and John served as the pastor of Ephesus for a time. Yet God did not prohibit them from becoming pastors due to their lack of education. So, the education rebuttal fails on multiple fronts.

Another two passages to consider are 1 Timothy 3:2 and Titus 1:6. In both of these chapters and verses, Paul is listing the qualifications of pastors. In those particular verses, he says that the pastor must be the husband of one wife, or literally a one-woman man. Now, that immediately disqualifies women from the pastorate, considering that they are not men, they are not husbands, and they are not a one-woman man. Based on those verses, here's what we have to say. We either have to say that only men can be pastors, or if women can be pastors, then there are literally no qualifications for them at all because all of the qualifications for pastors that we find in the Bible concern a one-woman man or the husband of one wife. Don't miss what I'm saying here. All of the qualifications for pastors in the Bible pertain to men, not women. So, if women can be pastors, there are absolutely no qualifications for them whatsoever.

Now, there are some common responses at this point that we need to address. When you look at the Bible and see that God clearly prohibits women from serving as pastors, people will sometimes point to the numerous examples of women serving in ministerial roles in Scripture as proof that women can be pastors. For instance, some people will say, well, look at Deborah. Deborah served as a judge in Israel. Yes, yes she did, but the role and position of a judge is not the same as the office of the pastor. So, the example of Deborah is not a good defense for making the case that women can be pastors today.

There are a few more examples that they point to. They'll say, well, women were the first to discover the empty tomb of Jesus and proclaim the resurrection of Jesus to others. Again, I hope you can see and understand that women discovering the empty tomb and then telling people that Jesus is alive is drastically different than serving in the office of pastor, so that's not a good example either. Another common response at this point is people will say that women served as prophets in the New Testament, such as Anna and the daughters of Philip. Other people will point to examples like how Priscilla was ministering along with her husband, Aquila. Again, though, I hope that we can see that serving as a prophet or ministering beside your husband, not in the position of a pastor, by the way, is not the same thing as serving in the office of the pastor. The office of the pastor is different than being a prophet, and the office of the pastor is different than having your wife come alongside you as a helper and assist you in your ministry. So, we aren't denying that women have been judges, prophets, and bold witnesses for Jesus. They have, and praise God for it. All we are saying is that the Bible limits the office of pastor to men.

So please understand this, folks: there isn't a Scriptural case that can be made for women pastors. Those in support of women pastors either have to ignore the clear teachings of Scripture or interpret them contrary to their plain meaning and twist them to make them mean whatever they want them to mean. Unfortunately, this is often when feelings get brought into the discussion. Some will say, well, this is sexist. This isn't fair. However, I don't believe that to be true. The fact that God has called men to be pastors and restricted women from being pastors is not in any way, shape, or form saying that men are better than women or men are more valuable than women. It simply means that God has a certain order for the church and for the roles of men and women in the church.

You can think about it like this. Let's say that I go to my local hardware store and purchase a $20 hammer and $20 garden shears. Then I go home to do some work. Well, if I want to go out and prune my garden or my shrubs, I won't grab the hammer. I mean, I can, and I can try to use it, but it's not what it's meant for. Does that mean that the hammer is less valuable than the shears? No, not at all. They both cost $20. It just means that each tool has its own task that it's best equipped to handle.

So, it is with men and women in the church. God has designed us and ordered His church in the way that He deemed best, not that humans deemed best, but that God deemed best. So, we're not denying that there are women who are incredibly gifted communicators. There are. We're not denying that there are women who have the ability to teach. There are. We're not denying that there are women with valuable insights into the Scriptures. There are. My wife, Anna, is one of these. She often will see things that I miss or that I overlook, or she'll bring out a point in a passage of Scripture that I haven't thought about in that way before. There are women with very valuable insights into the Scriptures. All we're saying is that the Bible limits and restricts the office of pastor to men as qualified by Scripture.

There are plenty of other important ways for women to serve and function in the church, and we're actually going to be addressing that and discussing that in a future question. I'm not going to spoil it now, but please understand this isn't a personal issue. It's not a matter of how we feel or what we think. It literally all comes down to what the Bible says. If we consider ourselves Christians, then we must submit ourselves to God and His rule as revealed in His inspired, inerrant, infallible Word. He alone is our ultimate authority, not our feelings, and certainly not the culture or the times. So let's please make sure that as Christians, we are basing all of our beliefs on what Scripture actually says, not what we want them to say, not what we twist them to mean, not what the culture says they can mean, but what the Scripture says clearly and plainly. So that's what the Bible says about who can serve as pastors.

Chapter 28

What's the Deal With She-Bears Killing Children?

✝

I love this question because it gets brought up from time to time when I'm talking with unbelievers. Typically, at some point when they're trying to show me how the Bible promotes evil and how God is evil, they'll say, didn't a bunch of bears kill children in the Bible? That's messed up. And hey, listen, that's a fair point. But is it really that simple? I mean, what actually happened in that situation?

If you're unfamiliar with the story that we're talking about, it occurs in the story of the prophet Elisha and is found in 2 Kings 2:23-25. This is what the Bible says, "He went up from there to Bethel. And while he was going up on the way, some small boys came out of the city and jeered at him, saying, go up, you bald head, go up, you bald head. And he turned around and when he saw them, he cursed them in the name of the Lord. And two she-bears came out of the woods and tore 42 of the boys. And there he went on to Mount Carmel and from there he returned to Samaria."

Now, admittedly, this story seems pretty straightforward, doesn't it? So, let's dive into some details to see if we can make sense of it. The most important thing to remember when you're trying to understand the Bible is **context is king**. I say this to my church all the time. You cannot properly interpret the Bible unless you understand the context of what you are reading. Context is king. Context determines meaning. So, let's first consider the historical context. What was going on at this point?

This story occurs at an important point in the history of Israel and in the life of Elisha. In order to really understand, we have to go all the way back to 1 Kings 19. Most of you will be familiar with this story because of the famous "still small voice." In 1 Kings 19, the prophet Elijah is on a mountain, and he is upset because he feels as though he alone is faithful to the Lord. He's complaining that all have abandoned God and that he alone is the only true believer. Now, it's important to remember that he's a prophet, and as a prophet, he is supposed to be interceding for the people. That is the role, part of the role at least, of a prophet. He is supposed to intercede to God on behalf of the people, but he is failing in that role, and instead, he's condemning everyone. He's saying, God, everybody is awful except for me. They're all just a bunch of no-good sinners. You should just be done with them all because I'm all you've got. He tells the Lord that he doesn't want to do this anymore. He wants to be done being a prophet. So then God speaks to him in a "still small voice," and he tells Elijah that even though he thinks he's the only faithful person left, God has a remnant of people. There are 7,000 people who have not bowed their knees to other gods and have not abandoned the Lord. So Elijah was wrong in understanding the situation, and he could have been interceding for at least 7,000 other people he was condemning.

The Lord accepts that he's done serving as a prophet, and He tells Elijah that he is to go and anoint two new kings and one new prophet. Now, this is a very important point. Elijah wished destruction on the people of Israel because he viewed them as a bunch of unfaithful sinners. What's going to happen is the Lord is essentially going to grant Elijah's wish because the two kings that he anoints and the new prophet that he anoints will be some of the most violent and deadly kings and prophets in the entire Bible. So Elijah goes, and he does as he's told. He anoints Hazael, king over Syria; he anoints Jehu, king over Israel (feel free at this point to go back and read about all that Jehu did and the bloodshed that he caused); and he anoints Elisha as the new prophet of God.

So then 1 Kings ends, and we come to 2 Kings. As 2 Kings starts, we get a description of Elijah's appearance. The Bible says that Elijah was a hairy man who wore a garment made out of hair (2 Kings 1:8). Right after we read about his appearance, we get this famous story in which God takes Elijah up into heaven. Elisha is with him at this point, and three separate times, Elijah says to Elisha, "Stay here." However, each time, Elisha responds by saying, I will never leave you (2 Kings 2:2, 4, 6). Then Elisha asks for a double portion of Elijah's spirit, and Elijah says, that's a hard request, but it's going to be done for him. Then we read about the chariots of fire and the horsemen who descend and grab Elijah. The Bible says that Elijah "went up by a whirlwind into heaven." (2 Kings 2:11)

This is the important background to note as we come to the She-Bear story. There are a few details that I want you to remember about this background. First, you need to remember Elijah's appearance. He was a really hairy person who even wore a garment of hair. Second, you need to remember that Elisha said he would never leave Elijah, but when Elijah *goes up*, Elisha cannot go with him. He stays behind. Finally, you need to remember that Elisha received a double portion of Elijah's spirit, meaning he should be twice the prophet that Elijah was. All of these details are going to be essential for understanding the She-Bear story.

Immediately after Elijah is taken up into heaven, Elisha demonstrates that he really is the new prophet of God and has the power and authority of that position by healing a contaminated spring of water. Immediately after that, we read the She-Bear story. They occur back-to-back in the Bible. However, there's one more bit of information we need to understand before we can fully understand the She-Bear story: the significance of the location in which it takes place.

The She-Bear story takes place in the city of Bethel. Bethel is significant in the Bible for many reasons, but at this point in Israel's history, the city had become the center of idolatry and false worship.[83] Shrines had been established in Bethel to rival Jerusalem. Essentially, the king wanted people to come and worship at the shrines he had set up in Bethel rather than go to Jerusalem to worship as the Lord commanded. Not only that, but Bethel was also well known at this point for establishing a prophetic school in the community that trained prophets who propagated false messages. These false prophets served the interest of the ruling establishment and supported the idolatrous practices that were common at the time. They were often seen as adversaries to true prophets like Elisha, who spoke on behalf of the Lord and called for repentance and fidelity to God's commands. All of this is the background to the She-Bear story.

With all this in mind, let's see if we can make sense of it now. Elisha, having been anointed the new prophet of God and given a double portion of Elisha's spirit, enters into Bethel, a city that has set itself against the Lord and His ways and has devoted itself to raising up false prophets. Upon entering the city, Elisha encounters what our English Bibles refer to as some "small boys." That's not a great translation. The Hebrew phrase that's actually used here indicates that these were not children at all. They were most likely young men in their late teens or early twenties who were students at the prophetic school in Bethel. So when you're thinking about this story, don't picture a bunch of elementary-age boys, but picture some college-age guys. That's the people he was dealing with here. When he encounters these college-age guys from this school of false prophets, they start mocking him, and they say, "Go up, you bald head, go up, you bald head."

So, let's just think about this. First, that's not a great insult, right? What's up with that insult? I mean, was Elisha bald? Who knows? Probably not, though. For instance, Elisha was a relatively young man at the time. He probably would have been in his late twenties or maybe early thirties. It would have been highly uncommon for him to be bald, but someone might say, well, maybe he shaved his head. Also, probably not because, at the time, prophets typically wore their hair long, like Elijah. Furthermore, prophets and many other holy men at the time would wear head coverings, especially considering they were in a very arid environment. So, even if he was bald, how could they tell?

When you begin to ask questions like these, you realize it's not actually about baldness. These mocks of "Go up, you bald head" are specifically tailored to call into question Elisha's authority and calling as the new prophet of God. You might be saying, well, where on earth did you get that? How do we know that? It's simple. Do you remember Elijah's appearance? I told you you would need to remember it. How does the Bible describe him? He was a really hairy man who even wore a garment of hair. When you think about Elijah, you think about hair. What's the opposite of hairy? Bald. So they're saying to him, "You're no Elijah."

Not only that, notice what else they're saying. "Go up, you bald head, go up." Why would they say that? Why say go up? What does that even mean? What's the significance of that? Well, remember, Elijah was taken *up* into heaven, and Elisha had told him, I will never leave you, but he was *unable* to go with him. So these young men are saying, "If you were really as holy as Elijah, if you were really a prophet like Elijah, and you really had a double portion of Elijah's spirit, then you could go up into heaven just as he did." But since he is here on earth and it seems as though he can't do that, they're saying once again, "You're no Elijah. You're no prophet of God."

Does this make sense now? Because they are false prophets from Bethel who are opposed to God in His ways, promote false teaching, and have no desire to recognize someone else as the true prophet of God, they make a taunt specifically aimed at undermining and calling into question Elisha's authority and position. "Go up, you bald head," which again is essentially saying, "You're no Elijah. You're no true prophet of God." How does the true prophet of God respond? Not well, admittedly. He demonstrates his authority as the prophet of God, and he does so violently, which, again, is why we talked about earlier that God was essentially granting Elijah's wish that God would just destroy the people. God does so by anointing violent kings and a violent new prophet. He's basically saying, "Okay, Elijah, if that's what you want, let me grant your wish for you. Here are the new kings of Israel. Here's the new prophet of God." The kings are violent, and even this prophet is violent. So Elisha, being the violent prophet that he is, curses the young men in the name of the Lord, and two she-bears come out and tear 42 of them.

It's important to note here that the Hebrew word for tore is *bāqa◇*. I've done a great deal of research on this. I cannot find one instance in the Bible where *bāqa◇* refers to killing or death at all. Usually, throughout the Bible, it means to rip open.[84] So we don't know if anyone died here. Maybe they did, maybe they didn't, but the Bible does not say here that these two she-bears came out and killed these young men. All we know for sure is that they were mauled and ripped open by the she-bears. It's their punishment for seeking to undermine God's ways and God's authority and for questioning the person that God specifically chose to be His new prophet.

So that's the she-bear story. It's very misunderstood today. It's very wrongly interpreted today. It is not God sending some she-bears to kill a bunch of children because God is some cruel or angry God. That's not it at all. It's a story about a bunch of college-age false prophets setting themselves against God and undermining and questioning Elisha's authority and position as the new prophet of God. They are saying if he were truly the new prophet with a double portion of Elisha's spirit, he would be able to go up into heaven now. Elisha responds by demonstrating his authority as the true prophet of God, and he does so in a violent way. So, I hope that this helps you understand the Bible better. I hope that this helps you understand this story better. Always remember to pay attention to the context. Context is king.

Chapter 29

What's the Significance of Jonah Sitting in a Booth on a Mountain?

✝

This question actually comes from one of our church members, I'm pretty sure because I preached a message on Jonah 4 called "God Loves People You Don't Like," and I said in the sermon that there was a lot of significance to Jonah sitting in a booth on a mountain but that I didn't really have time to get into all that.[85] So I said, hey, if anyone's interested, you can submit the question to the podcast, and I'm thankful someone did.

If you'll recall what's actually going on in Jonah 4, Jonah has finally and reluctantly warned the Ninevites of God's impending judgment, but to Jonah's great displeasure, the Ninevites actually listened and repented of their sins, and the Lord had mercy upon them. Then, in Jonah 4:1, literally in the Hebrew word-for-word, it reads, "But it was evil to Jonah, a great evil, and he burned with anger." Then, in verse five, we read this, "Jonah went out of the city and he sat to the east of the city and made a booth for himself there. He sat under it in the shade till he should see what would become of the city."

Now, immediately notice something significant we have already discussed in a previous question. Did you notice that Jonah went out to the east of the city? Remember, we said that throughout the Bible, whenever someone goes *to the East*, they're moving away from God and His will and toward disobedience. That's exactly what Jonah is doing here. He's not acting according to God's will and way. He's literally on this small mountain outside the city of Nineveh, waiting to see if God will judge Nineveh. He's actually wanting to have a good view to watch the city burn. That's how messed up this is. That's how far Jonah is from the heart of God at this moment. He wants to have a front-row seat and a high view so that he can watch this city burn.

As a prophet, he is not supposed to be acting this way. I mean, as a follower of God, he's not supposed to be acting this way, but especially as a prophet, he is supposed to be an intercessor for people, not a judge to condemn people. What you see here is Jonah failing in the prophetic role. Interestingly, this whole scenario of a prophet who is supposed to intercede for people, a prophet who's on a mountain after dealing with sinful people, actually appears as a pattern in Scripture. In order to see where it actually began, you have to go all the way back to Exodus chapter 32.

In Exodus 32, we get the prophetic ideal: what a prophet is supposed to do, who a prophet is supposed to be, and how a prophet is supposed to act when people do not do as God wants them to do. In the context of Exodus 32, the Lord had just delivered the Israelites from Egypt and called Moses up on Mount Sinai to receive the law. Let's pay attention to some details. You have a prophet on a mountain, but almost immediately after Moses goes up on the mountain, do you remember what happened? The people of Israel rebelled against the Lord and made a golden calf. Aaron, their priest, even looks at them and says, "These are your gods, O Israel, who brought you out of the land of Egypt" (Exodus 32:4). They end up worshiping this golden calf right after the Lord delivered them from Egypt, and Moses came down the mountain and sees what the people are doing. He sees that they have rebelled against God, and he is angry. He's so angry that he breaks the two tablets the Lord gave him (Exodus 32:19). He is in this fit of anger, and he's disappointed with the people. He has every opportunity here to be like Jonah would be later and ask the Lord to condemn the people, to pour out His wrath upon the people. Interestingly, God was actually preparing to do that. God was angry but notice what happens.

Exodus chapter 32:11-14, "But Moses implored the Lord his God and said, 'Oh Lord, why does your wrath burn hot against your people whom you have brought out of the land of Egypt with great power and with a mighty hand? Why should the Egyptians say with evil intent did he bring them out to kill them in the mountains and to consume them from the face of the earth? Turn from your burning anger and relent from this disaster against your people. Your Abraham, Isaac and Israel, your servants to whom you swore by your own self and said to them, I will multiply your offspring as the stars of heaven and all this land that I have promised I will give to your offspring and they shall inherit it forever. And the Lord relented from the disaster that he had spoken of bringing on his people."

I want you to pay attention here. This is setting up the ideal of what a prophet of God is supposed to be and what he is supposed to do. Prophets are supposed to *intercede for people*, not *condemn people*. Even though the people of Israel had immediately rebelled and sinned against the Lord and even though they did deserve His wrath, Moses pleaded their case before the Lord. He was begging the Lord to have mercy. That is what a prophet is supposed to do.

Then, something else interesting happens while Moses is on the mountain. While he is on Mount Sinai, Moses tells God that he wants to see His glory. You remember God responds and says, no one can see my face and live (Exodus 33:20). Then the Lord comes up with a plan. He says, here is what I am going to do. I am going to hide you in the cleft of a rock, which is essentially a cave. A cleft in a rock is what we typically refer to as a cave of sorts, and God says He is going to pass by so that Moses can see the backside of His glory as He passes by. Interestingly, right after the Lord does pass by and Moses does see the glory of God, Moses' face begins to shine, and he has to cover it. We need to keep all those details in mind as we continue to go throughout the Bible and see how this pattern is continued. Scripture establishes Moses as the prophetic ideal in terms of how a prophet is supposed to respond to the sinfulness of others: he is supposed to be an intercessor.

The next time this scenario takes place in Scripture, where another prophet has the opportunity to fulfill that ideal, but he fails, happens in 1 Kings 19. For context, remember that in this chapter, the prophet Elijah is on a mountain, just like Moses was. There is a good chance that Elijah is on Mount Sinai, the same mountain as Moses. Not only that, the Bible says that Elijah was in the cave. Your English translations there in 1 Kings 19:9 will say "a cave," but that is wrong. In Hebrew, it literally says Elijah was in "the cave."86 You might be saying, what is the big deal about that? You're getting hung up on A's and The's. Well, here's the big deal. Unlike Greek, Hebrew uses the definite article (the) very sparingly. You see it all the time in Greek, but in Hebrew, it's used very sparingly. So if Elijah is, in fact, on Mount Sinai, what would be the cave, this one very specific cave that it's referring to? Well, most likely, it's none other than the very cleft of the rock that Moses was in when he saw the glory of God.

Furthermore, remember why Elijah is on the mountain in the first place. He is on the run from Jezebel. He's on this mountain and angry because he feels as though he alone is faithful to the Lord. The Lord asked him what he was doing on the mountain, and this is how Elijah responded in 1 Kings 19:10. He says, "I have been very jealous for the Lord, the God of Hosts. For the people of Israel have forsaken your covenant, thrown down your altars and killed your prophets with a sword, and I, even I only am left, and they seek my life to take it away."

Notice the difference here. When Moses was on the mountain, he begged and pleaded with the Lord to have mercy on the people. He didn't say anything like, hey God, I'm the best person you have; I'm the only person you have. Moses didn't talk about himself at all. He was basing his plea for mercy on the Lord's covenant faithfulness. But that's not what Elijah does. He falls short of the prophetic ideal. He doesn't intercede for the people at all. He condemns them. He's essentially saying, Lord, they're all just a bunch of no-good sinners. You should be done with them because I'm all you have. However, the Lord responds in 1 Kings 19:11-12, "Go out and stand on the mount before the Lord. And behold, the Lord *passed by*." We'll continue with the verses, but think about how that sounds exactly like what happened in Exodus. You have Elijah, who's in this cave, most likely the same cave that Moses was in, and here you have the Lord *passing by*. The verses continue, "Behold, the Lord passed by, and a great and strong wind tore the mountains and broken pieces the rocks before the Lord. But the Lord was not in the wind. And after the wind, an earthquake. But the Lord was not in the earthquake. And after that earthquake, a fire. But the Lord was not in the fire. And after the fire, the sound of a low whisper," or the one you're most familiar with, a 'still small voice.'

All of these things indicate the presence of the Lord is there with Elijah. What's very interesting is immediately after this encounter with the Lord passing by Elijah and the still small voice and Elijah actually hearing the voice of God from heaven, the Bible says that Elijah covers his face. Why would he do that? Because, like Moses, he had seen God's glory and experienced God's presence, and just as Moses had to cover his face because it was shining, so too Elijah covers his face. It's almost the exact same scenario as Moses' situation on Sinai, but the difference is that Elijah falls short of the prophetic ideal.

Next, we come to Jonah. Jonah is yet another failure of the prophetic ideal because, again, recall the scene in Jonah and notice how similar it is to the previous two stories. We have a prophet who's on a mountain, which he went to after dealing with sinners. Like Elijah, he falls short of what he is supposed to be and do. Like Elijah, he is complaining about the people and wanting the Lord to condemn the people rather than interceding for them as he is supposed to as a prophet. Not just that, remember that Jonah is also in a booth on a mountain, a temporary dwelling place much like a cave was a temporary dwelling. It's not exactly a cave. He's not in some stone structure here but in a temporary dwelling, much like a cave. Not only that, but notice too that there's heat and there's wind just like in Elijah's situation, so much so that they're beating down on Jonah's head and face, meaning that if you were to look at Jonah, there is a physical, visible reaction to what Jonah is experiencing much like the shining faces of Moses and Elijah, not that is facing is actually shining, but there was a visible, physical reaction. Further, just like Moses and Elijah, Jonah hears the voice of God from heaven. So Moses is the ideal, while Elijah and Jonah fall short of the prophetic office.

Now, when you begin to look at those three stories, and you see the similarities, you see the themes that are being brought out, you see how Moses sets up the ideal, you see how Elijah and Jonah fall short, all of that is pretty cool to just look at in Scripture and say, hey, look at all these similarities. Clearly, there's a pattern going on here, but there's more than just one. There's actually a fulfillment of this theme and this pattern in Scripture. There's a fulfillment of the true prophet, and that takes us to the New Testament because, in the New Testament, we have another mountain story with a prophet going on a mountain and hearing the voice of God and having a shining face, just like in Moses's story and Elijah's story and in Jonah's story. It takes us to Matthew 17, where we get the famous story of Jesus's transfiguration.

Remember that leading up to this event, Jesus had been warning His disciples about the religious leaders of Israel (Matthew 16:5-12). Jesus was disappointed by their sinfulness and how they were continually leading his people astray. So, the initial setup is the same as the other incidents. People are in rebellion against the Lord, and now we see what the true prophet will do. He goes up on the mountain, and He takes with him Peter, James, and John. What happens on the mountain? Do you remember? The Bible says that Jesus was transfigured before them, and His face shone like the sun. Just as Moses's and Elijah's faces were shining from the glory of God, and just as Jonah was visibly affected by the presence of the Lord, Jesus's face began to shine, and His clothes became white as light.

Interestingly enough, who shows up at this meeting? This story is going to make so much more sense now that you've seen this pattern. Do you remember who shows up at this meeting when Jesus is on the mountain? It's none other than Moses and Elijah. What a coincidence, right? Many say that Moses and Elijah show up here as representations of the law and the prophets. There's certainly truth in that. I'm sure that's one of the main reasons they were there, but that explanation alone misses this huge pattern and theme of what the true prophet is supposed to be because the people that we have here meeting with Jesus on this mountain are the ideal prophet (Moses) and the first major prophet who failed to fulfill the ideal (Elijah).

It's at that point that Peter speaks up. Peter always speaks up and puts his foot in his mouth. He says, "Lord, it's good that we're here. If you wish, I will make three tents," (Matthew 17:4) or note this: tents is the exact same word for booths. Some of your translations might actually say booths. So he says, "I'll make three tents here, one for you and one for Moses and one for Elijah" (Matthew 17:4). Now, if you've ever read this story before and you've been confused by it, you might be wondering, well, why would he say that? Why would he want to make a booth? Why would he want to make booths for everybody who's there? Well, who else had a booth? Jonah. So Peter thinks, maybe like Jonah, we're meant to stay here. Peter's thinking, maybe we're going to stay up here, and maybe God will pour out His wrath on all those sinners below. Maybe He's going to send his wrath upon them, and we're going to get to stay up here and watch, and we're going to be kept safe from the wrath of God to come. So, even Peter is thinking along the lines of Elijah and Jonah rather than Moses.

Then everybody on the mountain hears, like Moses, Elijah, and Jonah, the voice of God from heaven. The Lord says, "This is my beloved son with whom I am well pleased. Listen to him" (Matthew 17:5). Neither Moses nor Elijah, nor Jonah had God say that about them. God did not say about any of them, this is my beloved son with whom I am well pleased. He only says that about Jesus because Jesus is the fulfillment of the prophetic office. We see that fulfillment in another way because after Moses came down from the mountain, Moses sinned against

God and was unable to enter the promised land or help the people do anything about their sin problem. After Elijah came down from the mountain, he gave up the prophetic office entirely, and he went and anointed a new prophet. So, he was unable to intercede any further or help the people out with their sin problem. We don't know what happened to Jonah when he came off the mountain, but based on his attitude, it's pretty safe to assume that he didn't and couldn't help the people with their sin problem. But what does Jesus do when He comes down off the mountain? The Bible tells us in Luke chapter 9 that Jesus "set his face to Jerusalem" (Luke 9:51), where He will suffer and die to intercede for His people in the greatest way possible and free His people from sin once and for all. Truly, He is the fulfillment of the true prophet of God.

So, we have to pay attention to the greater biblical story at all times. We must pay attention to biblical themes and patterns throughout Scripture. The story of Jonah on the mountain may seem strange at first, but when you realize that it's continuing a greater biblical theme and pattern, you begin to understand it better. You begin to understand that Jonah is yet another failed prophet falling short of the office and the ideal, and all of these failures by the prophets make us long for a greater prophet who will perfectly intercede for God's people and finally free God's people from the burden of sin. We finally get that fulfillment in Jesus' transfiguration, where we see that He is the true prophet of God who even supersedes the ideals set up by Moses, and He perfectly intercedes for His people and deals with the problem of sin. So that's the significance of Jonah sitting in a booth on a mountain.

Chapter 30

Are There Still
Prophets Today?

✝

That's a good question because it's fairly common in our day to see people refer to themselves as apostles or prophets. People who do this typically gain a lot of prominence and popularity because the title that they've given themselves is one that typically warrants respect. When people see someone who's called an apostle or a prophet or something like that, they tend to flock to them and give them a lot of attention and respect. But the question is, are there really still prophets today? In order to answer that question, we have to first define a prophet. What is a prophet?

According to the Bible, a true prophet is a person who receives direct, infallible revelation from God and proclaims that infallible message to others. All right, so think about that again. A true prophet is a person who receives direct, infallible revelation from God and then proclaims that infallible message to others. In the book of Deuteronomy, when the Lord is explaining to His people how to tell the difference between true prophets and false prophets, He says this in Deuteronomy

18:22, "When a prophet speaks in the name of the Lord, if the word does not come true, that is a word that the Lord has not spoken. The prophet has spoken it presumptuously." I want you to notice within that verse, we see the two aspects of our definition of a true prophet.

First, a true prophet must hear and proclaim only what the Lord has said to proclaim. He must not just proclaim something according to his will and desire and then try to pass it off as if the Lord revealed it to him. This means that true prophets must wait for the Lord to reveal to them the message they are to proclaim to others. This would be a direct revelation from God.

Then there's that second aspect of being a true prophet. The true prophet must not be proven wrong. This goes right along with only proclaiming what the Lord has revealed to the prophet because if God says something, it's true because God is truth. He is the source of all truth, and the Bible says in Numbers 23:19 that God is not a man that he should lie. It is impossible for God to lie. So then, every word that proceeds from the mouth of God is true and cannot be proven false, which means if the prophet is a true prophet and is really proclaiming to others what God has really revealed to him, then he will never be proven wrong. All of his prophecies will come true because he is speaking the very words of the Lord. However, false prophets will utter all sorts of prophecies that will clearly be shown to be false. Therefore, according to the Bible, a true prophet is a person who receives direct, infallible revelation from God and then proclaims that infallible message to others.

Throughout the Bible, we see both true prophets and false prophets. There were those to whom the Lord actually did appear and give direct, infallible revelation that was intended to be proclaimed to others, but then there were also those who claimed to be prophets and claimed to speak on behalf of the

Lord but were actually false prophets. It never ended well for the false prophets. I hope you hear me on this. It is a dangerous thing to claim to have heard from the Lord and speak for the Lord if that is not the case. For instance, when the Lord was addressing the false prophets in Jeremiah's day and saying what He was going to do to them, He said in Jeremiah 14:15, "By sword and famine, those prophets shall be consumed." In other words, the false prophets will be met with the wrath of God for spreading lies, leading people astray, and claiming to speak for God when He had not said anything to them.

Of course, we know that prophets didn't just exist in the Old Testament but continued into the New Testament times. However, what we need to understand is that the prophets during the New Testament times, especially those who were prophets after the resurrection and ascension of Jesus, served a very particular function. They were there for a very particular reason, which brings us to our discussion of whether there are still prophets today. It all is going to hinge and depend upon the role or purpose of prophets. What role do they play in the life of the church? Why did God give prophets in the first place? We need to see the role that they actually played when it came to the church.

We see the purpose of prophets in Ephesians 2:19- 20. The Bible says this, "So then you are no longer strangers and aliens, but you are fellow citizens with the saints and members of the household of God, built on the foundation of the apostles and prophets, Christ Jesus Himself being the cornerstone." Notice what the Bible is saying there. The Bible specifically says that the church is built on the *foundation* of the Apostles and prophets, with Jesus being the cornerstone. Very plain and simple: the Apostles and prophets were meant to serve as the foundation of the church. They were supposed to be that foundation upon which everything else in the church was built. So let me ask you this question: Is the foundation complete?

Has the foundation already been laid? If it hasn't, does that mean that no building has been done in the church since Jesus's ascension? If we're saying that the foundation is not completed, then that means nothing's being built because you can't build unless you have a completed foundation. You have no security and strength of structure without a foundation. So my question again is, has the foundation been completed? Has it already been laid?

As you're thinking about that, and before we answer it, let me ask you another important question on this topic. In what way did the Apostles and prophets serve as the foundation? It's one thing to say that they served as the church's foundation, but what does that mean? In what way did they serve as the foundation? Well, I want you to think through what those offices actually are. They are the revelation-bearing offices of the church. That's what the Apostles were. That's what the prophets were. They were the revelation-bearing offices of the church. In other words, God revealed His Word through the Apostles and prophets. Ultimately, the Word of God is the foundation of the church, but the Apostles and prophets can be said to be its foundation because they were the ones who revealed and proclaimed that Word to the world.

So think about it like this, then. If the Apostles and prophets served as the foundation of the church, and the way in which they served as the foundation of the church was by being the revelation-bearing office of the church and bringing God's Word to the people, we need to consider this then. In order for the foundation to be complete, that means the Word of God would have to be complete, right? If the Word of God is ultimately the foundation of the church, then for that foundation to be complete, the Word of God would have to be complete. So let me ask you this question: Has the Word of God been completed?

The answer is yes. We know that the canon was closed nearly 2,000 years ago. Not only that, we read in Hebrews 1:1-2, "Long ago, at many times and in many ways God spoke to our fathers by the prophets, but in these last days He has spoken to us by His Son." In other words, the Bible is saying that Jesus is God's full and final revelation, that He is God's final revelation to the world, the culmination of God's revelation. We know that the life and words of Jesus are recorded for us in the Bible. So, with the completion of the Bible, we also have the completion of the foundation.

So let's think about this again, going all the way back to the passage from Ephesians that says that the church is built on the foundation of the Apostles and the prophets, and we see that they were the revelation-bearing offices of the church, bringing God's Word to the world. Since the Bible has been completed, since the canon is closed and the foundation has been laid, it means that we no longer have a *need* for prophets or Apostles. They have served their God-intended purpose. Therefore, there are no more Apostles or prophets today.

It's important that we get clear on this issue because there's a lot of confusion about it today and a lot of opportunity for confusion. For instance, it's quite common today for people to say something like, "God told me..." This is essentially on par with claiming to have received a prophetic word from the Lord. It's essentially claiming that, like a prophet, you have received direct revelation from God. You are saying, God told me this thing. However, there are a lot of issues with such statements.

First, a person who says this is claiming like a prophet, as we just said, to have received a direct word from the Lord. If that is true, if the Lord actually did say something to this person, then that word is true and infallible. But not only that, it comes from the Lord. So, it would be on par with Scripture because both come from the Lord and are infallible. But we know, as we just said, that the Scriptures have been completed now for approximately 2,000 years. So here's my question: Anytime someone says, well, the Lord told me this or God said this to me, are we supposed to reopen the canon every time someone says that? Are we supposed to then add the words to the Scriptures that we have today? If God said something to John Smith, are we supposed to add that statement to the Bible then? If we're not supposed to add it to the Bible, you have to then say, well, why shouldn't we add it to the Bible? If it is from the Lord, and we know that because it's from the Lord, it is true and it is infallible, then why would we not add it to the Bible? You see, this is one of the biggest problems with these kinds of statements is they don't think about the implications of what such statements would mean for the entire church.

Another issue with such statements is that people will often use such statements for personal and selfish reasons. It's kind of like the ultimate trump card, isn't it? I mean, for instance, if you don't like something the pastor is doing at your church, you could simply say, well, God told me he doesn't like what you're doing; if the pastor disagrees, then that person can claim that the pastor is going against God. Listen to me, folks that is manipulative. I have seen such statements used by manipulative people who are seeking to control the church, who are seeking to have their ways and their will done in the church. They use God as a tool for their own selfish means. That is dangerous.

Not only that, but that's also how false religions and cults get started. I mean, just think about Mormonism, for instance. Joseph Smith claimed to have received new revelation from God that is on par with Scripture, so he started a brand new religion on that basis. Because people believed that he had actually received this word from God, they took it as gospel truth. They ran with it, and now they hold the teachings of Joseph Smith to be on par with the Bible, just as reliable as the Bible because he claims it comes from God.

Going along with this point, people will often claim that God told them something that directly contradicts Scripture, and there we have a huge issue, folks. When someone claims that God told them something that directly contradicts what is recorded in Scripture, we have no clue what to trust. I know of a situation where a man claimed that God told him it was okay for him to divorce his wife since he didn't love her anymore. He said God told me he wants me to be happy, and I'm not happy anymore, so he said it's okay for me to get a divorce. The problem is God's word says that God hates divorce and only allows for it in two very drastic circumstances. In that situation, who are we to believe if Scripture and the message that this man said he received from the Lord were from God? How do we judge which one is true and which one is not? Does God contradict himself? No, absolutely not. Does God say anything that's untrue? No. We would again have to go back to Scripture as our ultimate authority and say that if someone claims God told them something that goes against what we find in the inerrant, infallible, inspired, revealed Word of God that is Scripture, that person is lying.

It's not just divorce. There's a whole number of issues that people have often claimed that God told them it's okay for them to do that contradicts Scripture. We don't have time to get into all of them but suffice to say, if anyone ever says that God told them it's okay for them to do something that goes against what we read in Scripture, that person is lying because God does not contradict himself. It's as my favorite theologian of all time, John Owen, once said, "If private revelations agree with Scripture, they're unnecessary, and if they disagree, they're false."

That's one of our biggest issues today is everybody wants to receive a new word from the Lord. They want to hear from God, but God has already spoken to us. He has spoken to us in the most perfect way possible. He has spoken to us by His

Son, and that is recorded for us in Scripture. We do not need a new word for the Lord. It's amazing how often people say they want to hear from God, yet they don't go to the revealed Word that He has already given us. They say they want to hear from God but never open their Bibles. They say they want a word from the Lord but neglect the Word He's already given us. "If private revelations agree with Scripture, they're unnecessary; if they disagree, they're false."

Even though God doesn't speak audibly to people today or give new revelations today, He still gives impressions and leads people today. A person might sense that God is impressing upon him to speak to a coworker about Jesus. Or a person might sense that God is leading her to join a women's Bible study. Or a couple praying together might sense that the Lord is leading them to sell all they have and become missionaries to Taiwan. In these situations, it wouldn't be appropriate to say, "The Lord told me," since no words were spoken. However, it is entirely appropriate and biblical to say, "The Lord is leading me," or "The Lord has impressed upon me the need to"...The Lord does still work in these ways, but He does not give new revelation.

So, taking all that into consideration, we conclude that there are no more prophets today. With the conclusion of Scripture came the conclusion of God's prophetic Word. There are no more revelations from God because we have in Jesus God's full and final revelation, and that revelation is Scripture. Scripture is our ultimate authority. So, if you are looking for a word from the Lord or want to hear from God, read your Bibles.

Acknowledgments

I want to say a special thank you to Alejandro, John, and Emily for their help in making this book possible. Their work on the cover, formatting, and file conversion was invaluable. Thank you all!

End Notes

1. ^ Hebrew= 'āman, meaning believe or have faith. See Francis Brown, S.R. Driver, and Charles A. Briggs, A Hebrew and English Lexicon of the Old Testament (Oxford: Clarendon Press, 1907), H539 ◇n◇ 'āman.
2. ^ Brown-Driver-Briggs, H2803 ḥāšaḇ.
3. ^ Leon Morris, *The Gospel According to St. Luke: An Introduction and Commentary*, Tyndale New Testament Commentaries (Grand Rapids: Eerdmans, 1974), 253.
4. ^ Joseph Henry Thayer, Thayer's Greek-English Lexicon of the New Testament: Coded with the Numbering System from Strong's Exhaustive Concordance of the Bible (Peabody, MA: Hendrickson, 1996), G728 ἀρραβών.
5. ^ Thayer, G1100 γλῶσσα glōssa.
6. ^ Jamie George, *Poets and Saints: Eternal Insight. Extravagant Love. Ordinary People.* (Colorado Springs, Colorado: David C Cook, 2016), 25.
7. ^ George, *Poets and Saints*, 21; 25-26.
8. ^ George, 26.
9. ^ George, 27.
10. ^ George, 28-31.
11. ^ George, 31.
12. ^ George, 31-32.
13. ^ George, 33-35.
14. ^ George, 35.
15. ^ Michael Svigel and John Adair, *Urban Legends of Church History: 40 Common Misconceptions* (Nashville: B&H Academic, 2020), 39.
16. ^ Svigel and Adair, *Urban Legends of Church History*, 39.
17. ^ Timothy Paul Jones, How We Got the Bible (Peabody, Ma: Rose Publishing, 2015), 51-52).
18. ^ In 2 Peter 3:16, "scripture" = graphē, which always refers to Scripture throughout the New Testament.

19. ^ Michael J. Kruger, *Canon Revisited: Establishing the Origins and Authority of the New Testament Books* (Wheaton, IL: Crossway, 2012), 216-19.
20. ^ Michael Svigel and John Adair, 43.
21. ^ Svigel and Adair, *Canon Revisited*, 43.
22. ^ Svigel and Adair, 44.
23. ^ Svigel and Adair, 44.
24. ^ Svigel and Adair, 39.
25. ^ J. Scott Duvall, *Revelation* (Grand Rapids, MI: Baker Books, 2014), Teach the Text Commentary Series, 83.
26. ^ J. Scott Duvall, Revelation, 83.
27. ^ Jonathan Pennington, Come & See: The Journey of Knowing God Through Scripture (Wheaton, IL: Crossway, 2023), 15-16.
28. ^ Gregg R. Allison, Roman Catholic Theology and Practice: An Evangelical Assessment (Wheaton, IL: Crossway, 2014), 331.
29. ^ Sam Storms, "666-Revelation 13:11-18," samstorms.org, accessed October 10, 2023, Sam Storms: Oklahoma City, OK > 666 - Revelation 13:11-18.
30. ^ G. K. Beale, *The Book of Revelation: A Commentary on the Greek Text* (Grand Rapids, MI: Eerdmans, The New International Greek Testament Commentary, 1999), 719.
31. ^ Beale, *The Book of Revelation*, 719.
32. ^ Beale, 719.
33. ^ Thomas R. Schreiner, *The Joy of Hearing: A Theology of the Book of Revelation* (Wheaton, IL: Crossway, New Testament Theology Series, 2021), 53-61.
34. ^ Richard D. Phillips, *Revelation* (Phillipsburg, NJ: P&R Publishing, Reformed Expository Commentary Series, 2017), 383.
35. ^ Gregory Koukl, *Tactics: A Game Plan For Discussing Your Christian Convictions* (Grand Rapids, MI: Zondervan, 2009), 49-52.
36. ^ "Second Law of Thermodynamics," All About Science, accessed October 13, 2023, Second Law of Thermodynamics (allaboutscience.org).
37. ^ Andrew May, "Hubble's law: Why are most galaxies moving away from us?" Space.com, accessed October 13, 2023, Hubble's law: How we know galaxies are moving apart | Space.
38. ^ Wintery Knight, "How the Discovery of Cosmic Microwave Background Radiation Falsified Atheism," Cross Examined, accessed October 13, 2023, How The Discovery Of The Cosmic Microwave Background Radiation Falsified Atheism (crossexamined.org).
39. ^ *Expelled: No Intelligence Allowed.* Directed by Nathan Frankowski. Los Angeles, CA: Premise Media Corporation, 2008.

40. ^ "The Origins of the Universe l Peter Atkins," The Institute of Arts and Ideas, YouTube video, The Institute of Arts and Ideas, May 5, 2019, (25) The Origins of the Universe | Peter Atkins - YouTube.

41. ^ "The Origins of the Universe l Peter Atkins."

42. ^ Lawrence M. Krauss, Universe From Nothing: Why There Is Something Rather than Nothing (New York: Free Press, 2012).

43. ^ Stephen Hawking and Leonard Mlodinow, *The Grand Design* (New York: Bantam Books, 2010), 180.

44. ^ Committee on the Limits of Organic Life in Planetary Systems, Committee on the Origins and Evolution of Life, National Research Council, *The Limits of Organic Life in Planetary Systems*, 60.

45. ^ Harold G. Kofahl and Kelly L. Segraves, *The Creation Explanation* (Wheaton, IL: Harold Shaw Publishers, 1975), 101.

46. ^ C.P. Hickman, L.S. Roberts, and F. M. Hickman, Integrated Principles of Zoology (Times Mirror/Mosby College Publishing, 1988, 8th ed.), 866.

47. ^ Stephen C. Meyer, "The Cambrian Explosion," accessed October 2, 2023, The Cambrian Explosion | Stephen C. Meyer (stephencmeyer.org).

48. ^ "Irreducible Complexity: The Challenge to the Darwinian Evolutionary Explanations of many Biochemical Structures" IDEA Center, accessed October 2, 2023, Irreducible Complexity: The Challenge to the Darwinian Evolutionary Explanations of many Biochemical Structures (ideacenter.org).

49. ^ "Irreducible Complexity."

50. ^ Charles Darwin, *On the Origin of the Species* (London: John Murray, 1859), 189.

51. ^ Timothy Paul Jones, *How We Got the Bible*, 142.

52. ^ Jones, 142.

53. ^ Jones, 142.

54. ^ Shari Abbott, "Is Satan's Real Name Lucifer? Or Should We Call Him Satan?" Reasons For Hope, accessed October 10, 2023, Is Satan's real name Lucifer? Or should we call him Satan? (reasonsforhopejesus.com).

55. ^ Abbott, Reasons For Hope.

56. ^ Thayer, G444.

57. ^Teleological comes from *telos*. See Thayer, G5056.

58. ^ Stephen Hawking, *A Brief History of Time: From the Big Bang to Black Holes* (New York: Bantam Books, 1988), 162, 164.

59. ^ "The Anthropic Principle," May 18, 1987, Episode 17, Season 23, *Horizon* Series, BBC.

60.   ^ "ID's Top Six: The Fine-Tuning of the Universe," accessed October 2, 2023, ID's Top Six — The Fine-Tuning of the Universe | Evolution News.

61.   ^ "ID's Top Six."

62.   ^ "What Do Fine-Tuning and the Multiverse Say About God?" accessed October 2, 2023, What Do "Fine-tuning" and the "Multiverse" Say About God? - BioLogos.

63.   ^ "What Do Fine-Tuning and the Multiverse Say About God?"

64.   ^Obaidur Rahman, "The Anthropic Principle," The Daily Star, accessed October 16, 2023, https://www.thedailystar.net/news-detail-207808.

65.   ^ AP Staff, "The Earth- Our 'Just Right' Planet," Apologetics Press, accessed October 13, 2023, The Earth—Our "Just Right" Planet - Apologetics Press.

66.   ^ Doug Powell, "Does God Exist? (Part 2 of 4)," North American Mission Board, accessed October 13, 2023, Does God Exist? (Part 2 of 4) - Apologetics (namb.net).

67.   ^ "What does the anthropic principle demonstrate?" Compelling Truth, accessed October 13, 2023, What does the anthropic principle demonstrate? (compellingtruth.org).

68.   ^ Ibid.

69.   ^ Robert C. Stallman, "נחש" in The New International Dictionary of Old Testament Theology and Exegesis, ed. Willem VanGemeren, 5 vols. (Grand Rapids, MI: Zondervan, 1997), 3:85.

70.   ^ Brown-Driver-Briggs, H7193.

71.   ^ "Pope," Encyclopedia Britannica, accessed October 10, 2023, Pope | Definition, Title, List of Popes, & Facts | Britannica.

72.   ^ "Pope," Britannica.

73.   ^ Pat MCClosky, "Why Is the Pope Called the 'Supreme Pontiff'"? Franciscan Media, accessed October 10, 2023, Why Is the Pope Called the 'Supreme Pontiff'? | Franciscan Media.

74.   ^ "Pope," Britannica.

75.   ^ Martyn Whittock, "John Nelson Darby: the Man Who Popularised Dispensationalism," Christianity Today, accessed October 10, 2023, John Nelson Darby: the man who popularised dispensationalism (christiantoday.com).

76.   ^ Stephen Nichols, "Dispensationalism," *5 Minutes in Church History*, Ligonier Ministries, accessed [Insert Access Date], [Insert URL].

77.   ^ Whittock, "John Nelson Darby."

78.   ^ Anthony A. Hoekema, *The Bible and the Future* (Grand Rapids: Eerdmans, 1979), 164-165.

79. ^ John R. W. Scott, *The Message of 1 & 2 Thessalonians* (The Bible Speaks Today; Downers Grove: Intervarsity Press, 1982), 103.

80. ^ F. F. Bruce, *1 & 2 Thessalonians* (Word Biblical Commentary; Word, 1982), 102.

81. ^ "What is Karma?" Hindu American Foundation, accessed October 10, 2023, KarmaMokshaandSamsara2.0_0.pdf (hinduamerican.org).

82. ^ "What is Karma?" Hindu American Foundation.

83. ^ Maura Sala, "Bethel North of Jerusalem," in *Lexham Bible Dictionary* (Bellingham, WA: Lexham Press, 2016).

84. ^ Brown-Driver-Briggs, H1234.

85. ^ You can find that sermon here: God Loves People You Don't Like- Jonah 4 - georgescreekbaptist.org.

86. ^ Hebrew= המערה as opposed to מערה.

Selected Bibliography

Abbott, Shari. "Is Satan's Real Name Lucifer? Or Should We Call Him Satan?" Reasons For Hope. Accessed October 10, 2023. https://reasonsforhopejesus.com/is-satans-real-name-lucifer-or-should-we-call-him-satan/.

All About Science. "Second Law of Thermodynamics." Accessed October 13, 2023. https://www.allaboutscience.org/second-law-of-thermody-namics.htm.

Allison, Gregg R. *Roman Catholic Theology and Practice: An Evangelical Assessment.* Wheaton, IL: Crossway, 2014.

AP Staff. "The Earth- Our 'Just Right' Planet." Apologetics Press. Accessed October 13, 2023. https://apologeticspress.org/the-earthour-just-right-planet-3359/.

Beale, G.K. *The Book of Revelation: A Commentary on the Greek Text.* The New International Greek Testament Commentary. Grand Rapids, MI: Eerdmans, 1999.

Bio-Logos. "What Do Fine-Tuning and the Multiverse Say About God?" accessed October 2, 2023. https://biologos.org/common-questions/what-do-fine-tuning-and-the-multiverse-say-about-god.

Brown, Francis, S.R. Driver, and Charles A. Briggs. *A Hebrew and English Lexicon of the Old Testament.* Oxford: Clarendon Press, 1907.

Bruce, F. F. *1 & 2 Thessalonians.* Word Biblical Commentary. Word, 1982.

Compelling Truth. "What Does the Anthropic Principle Demonstrate?" accessed October 13, 2023. https://www.compellingtruth.org/anthropic-principle.html.

Darwin, Charles. *On the Origin of the Species*. London: John Murray, 1859.

Duvall, J. Scott. *Revelation*. Teach the Text Commentary Series. Grand Rapids, MI: Baker Books, 2014.

"Expelled: No Intelligence Allowed." Directed by Nathan Frankowski. Los Angeles, CA: Premise Media Corporation, 2008.

George, Jamie. *Poets and Saints: Eternal Insight. Extravagant Love. Ordinary People.* Colorado Springs, Colorado: David C. Cook, 2016.

Hawking, Stephen. *A Brief History of Time: From the Big Bang to Black Holes*. New York: Bantam Books, 1988.

Hawking, Stephen and Leonard Mlodinow. *The Grand Design*. New York, Bantam Books, 2010.

Hickman, C.P, L.S. Roberts, and F.M. Hickman. *Integrated Principles of Zoology, 8th ed.* Times Mirror/Mosby College Publishing, 1988.

Hoekema, Anthony A. *The Bible and the Future*. Grand Rapids, MI: Eerdmans, 1979.

IDEA Center. "Irreducible Complexity: The Challenge to the Darwinian Evolutionary Explanations of Many Biochemical Structures." accessed October 2, 2023. http://www.ideacenter.org/stuff/contentmgr/files/9147e04fc268407ac48a8915b73ef8e2/miscdocs/irreduciblecomplexity.pdf.

"ID's Top Six: The Fine-Tuning of the Universe." accessed October 2, 2023. https://evolutionnews.org/2017/11/ids-top-six-the-fine-tuning-of-the-universe/.

Jones, Timothy Paul. *How We Got the Bible*. Peabody, MA: Rose Publishing, 2015.

Knight, Wintery. "How the Discovery of Cosmic Background Radiation Falsified Atheism." Accessed October 13, 2023. https://crossexamined.org/how-the-discovery-of-the-cosmic-microwave-background-radiation-falsified-atheism/.

Kofahl, Harold G. and Kelly L. Segraves. *The Creation Explanation.* Wheaton, IL: Harold Shaw Publishers, 1975.

Koukl, Gregory. *Tactics: A Game Plan For Discussing Your Christian Convictions.* Grand Rapids, MI: Zondervan, 2009.

Krauss, Lawrence M. *A Universe From Nothing: Why There is Something Rather Than Nothing.* New York, Free Press, 2012.

Kruger, Michael J. *Canon Revisited: Establishing the Origins and Authority of the New Testament Books.* Wheaton, IL: Crossway, 2012.

May, Andrew. "Hubble's law: Why are most galaxies moving away from us?" Accessed October 13, 2023. https://www.space.com/hubbles-law.

McClosky, Pat. "Why is the Pope Called the 'Supreme Pontiff'"? Franciscan Media. Accessed October 10, 2023. https://www.franciscanmedia.org/ask-a-franciscan/why-is-the-pope-called-the-supreme-pontiff/.

Meyer, Stephen C. "The Cambrian Explosion." accessed October 2, 2023. https://stephencmeyer.org/2001/01/01/the-cambrian-explosion/.

Morris, Leon. *The Gospel According to St. Luke: An Introduction and Commentary.* Tyndale New Testament Commentaries. Grand Rapids: Eerdmans, 1974.

National Research Council. *The Limits of Organic Life in Planetary Systems.* Committee on the Origins and Evolution of Life.

Nichols, Stephen. "Dispensationalism," *5 Minutes in Church History.* Ligonier Ministries. Accessed October 10, 2023. https://www.ligonier.org/podcasts/5-minutes-in-church-history-with-stephen-nichols/dispensationalism.

Pennington, Jonathan. *Come & See: The Journey of Knowing God Through Scripture.* Wheaton, IL: Crossway, 2023.

Phillips, Richard D. *Revelation*. Reformed Expository Commentary Series. Phillipsburg, NJ: P&R Publishing, 2017.

"Pope." Encyclopedia Britannica. Accessed October 10, 2023. https://www.britannica.com/topic/pope.

Powell, Doug. "Does God Exist? (Part 2 of 4)." North American Mission Board. Accessed October 13, 2023. https://www.namb.net/apologetics/resource/does-god-exist-part-2-of-4/.

Rahman, Obaidur. "The Anthropic Principle." The Daily Star. Last updated October 25, 2011. Accessed October 16, 2023. www.dailystar.net/news-detail-207808.

Sala, Maura. "Bethel North of Jerusalem." *Lexham Bible Dictionary*. Bellingham, WA: Lexham Press, 2016.

Schreiner, Thomas R. *The Joy of Hearing: A Theology of the Book of Revelation*. New Testament Theology Series. Wheaton, IL: Crossway, 2021.

Stallman, Robert C. "נחש." *New International Dictionary of Old Testament Theology and Exegesis*, edited by Willem VanGemeren, 5 vols. Grand Rapids, MI: Zondervan, 1997.

Storms, Sam. "666-Revelation 13:11-18." Accessed October 10, 2023. https://www.samstorms.org/all-articles/post/666--revelation-1311-18.

Stott, John R. W. *The Message of 1 & 2 Thessalonians*. The Bible Speaks Today Commentary Series. Downers Grove, Intervarsity Press, 1982.

Svigel, Michael and John Adair. *Urban Legends of Church History: 40 Common Misconceptions*. Nashville: B&H Academic, 2020.

Thayer, Joseph Henry. *Thayer's Greek-English Lexicon of the New Testament: Coded with the Numbering System from Strong's Exhaustive Concordance of the Bible*. Peabody, MA: Hendrickson, 1996.

"The Anthropic Principle." May 18, 1987, Episode 17, Season 23, *Horizon Series*, BBC.

"The Origins of the Universe | Peter Atkins," The Institute of Arts and Ideas, YouTube video, May 5, 2019. https://www.youtube.com/watch?v=tSlL1UPrCOU&t=8s.

"What is Karma?" Hindu American Foundation. Accessed October 10, 2023. https://www.hinduamerican.org/wp-content/uploads/2019/12/KarmaMokshaandSamsara2.0_0.pdf.

Whittock, Martyn. "John Nelson Darby: The Man Who Popularised Dispensationalism." Christianity Today. Accessed October 10, 2023. https://www.christiantoday.com/article/john-nelson-darby-the-man-who-popularised-dispensationalism/140511.htm.

About the Author

 Rev. R. Alex Chapman serves as the Senior Pastor of Georges Creek Baptist Church in Easley, SC. He is married to his best friend, Anna, and the father of two sons, Judah and Ezra. Alex graduated from North Greenville University with a B.A. in Christian Studies and from The Southern Baptist Theological Seminary with an M.Div. in Christian Ministry.

 In addition to serving as the Senior Pastor of Georges Creek, Alex also helps develop Bible study curriculum for LifeWay Christian Resources by serving as a content and theology editor for their adult small group and Bible studies. He's also the host of the Ask Pastor Alex Podcast. For more information, please visit georgescreekbaptist.org.

Milton Keynes UK
Ingram Content Group UK Ltd.
UKHW010642271123
433342UK00003B/43